The Garden of Scripture

The Garden of Scripture

Growing Your Confidence in the Bible

TIM TSCHIDA

Foreword by Stacey Rose

RESOURCE *Publications* • Eugene, Oregon

THE GARDEN OF SCRIPTURE
Growing Your Confidence in the Bible

Copyright © 2025 Tim Tschida. All rights reserved. Except for brief quotations in critical publications or reviews, no part of this book may be reproduced in any manner without prior written permission from the publisher. Write: Permissions, Wipf and Stock Publishers, 199 W. 8th Ave., Suite 3, Eugene, OR 97401.

Resource Publications
An Imprint of Wipf and Stock Publishers
199 W. 8th Ave., Suite 3
Eugene, OR 97401

www.wipfandstock.com

PAPERBACK ISBN: 979-8-3852-3777-7
HARDCOVER ISBN: 979-8-3852-3778-4
EBOOK ISBN: 979-8-3852-3779-1

03/13/25

The Scripture contained herein are from the New Revised Standard Version, Updated Edition Bible, copyright © 1989, 2021 by the Division of Christian Education of the National Council of Churches of Christ in the U.S.A., and are used by permission. All rights reserved.
Scripture quotations labeled ESV are from The Holy Bible, English Standard Version® (ESV®), copyright © 2001 by Crossway, a publishing ministry of Good News Publishers. Used by Permission. All rights reserved.
Scripture quotations marked CSB have been taken from the Christian Standard Bible®, Copyright © 2017 by Holman Bible Publishers. Used by permission. Christian Standard Bible® and CSB® are federally registered trademarks of Holman Bible Publishers.
Scripture quotations marked (NIV) are taken from the Holy Bible, New International Version®, NIV®. Copyright © 1973, 1978, 1984, 2011 by Biblica, Inc.™ Used by permission of Zondervan. All rights reserved worldwide. www.zondervan.comThe "NIV" and "New International Version" are trademarks registered in the United States Patent and Trademark Office by Biblica, Inc.™

For my students

My soul is satisfied as with a rich feast,
    and my mouth praises you with joyful lips
when I think of you on my bed
    and meditate on you in the watches of the night,
for you have been my help,
    and in the shadow of your wings I sing for joy.
My soul clings to you;
    your right hand upholds me.

—Psalm 63:5–8 (NRSVUE)

Contents

Foreword by Stacey Rose — ix
Acknowledgments — xi
Scripture Abbreviations — xiii
Introduction — xv

1. A Storm of Perfection — 1
2. Prayer and the Spirit — 16
3. Embracing The Strange — 27
4. Illusions and Fullness — 42
5. A Disruptive God — 57
6. The Cloud — 71
7. Behold The Man! — 85
8. An Invitation To Slay Dragons — 107

Bibliography — 121

Foreword

THERE ARE FEW PEOPLE I trust as deeply to guide others in their Biblical studies as I do Tim Tschida. Over the years, I've watched him not only teach our students but disciple them with an authenticity that calls them into a deeper, more open walk with Christ. Tim isn't just a teacher; he is a mentor, a scholar, and—if you spend any time with him—a walking Biblical encyclopedia. I have never known anyone who can recall Scripture with the precision and depth that he does. But unlike an encyclopedia, Tim's teaching comes with a humility and a vulnerability that inspires.

This book, *The Garden of Scripture*, is a testament to Tim's remarkable ability to connect theological truths with the modern Christian life. Through insightful discussion, a wealth of research drawn from learned theologians, and fictional accounts that bring Biblical concepts and parables into a relatable, modern light, Tim has woven together a work that is both intellectual and deeply pastoral without the self-importance that distances the work from the reader.

One of the most striking aspects of this book is Tim's ability to tackle real issues and place them within the broader context of Christian history and theology. Whether he is referencing the transformative allegory of Eustace and his "undragoning" in C. S. Lewis's *The Voyage of the Dawn Treader*, or challenging the reader to meditate on Scripture in a way that counters today's new-age embrace of the "mystical," Tim brings clarity to the practicalities of living out the faith.

For me, one of the most poignant takeaways from this book is its call to embrace the disruptions caused by an authentic

Foreword

surrender to Christ. Tim doesn't shy away from the uncomfortable truths that come with discipleship—truths that require us to let go of our illusions of control and allow the Holy Spirit to sanctify and renew us while pushing us into uncomfortable spaces for our good.

The Garden of Scripture is more than a book; it is an invitation. An invitation to wrestle with the Word, to see Biblical truths through a fresh lens, and to grow in understanding the depth and breadth of God's redemptive plan. Whether you're a seasoned theologian or someone seeking to better understand the Bible's relevance today, you will find something here to challenge, inspire, and enrich your walk with the Lord.

It is my privilege to commend Tim Tschida's work to you. As you turn these pages, I hope you will see the same wisdom, passion, and commitment to truth that I see in Tim every day. May this book help you cultivate your own garden of Scripture—one that grows deeper roots, bears lasting fruit, and reflects the beauty of Christ's transformative power.

With gratitude and anticipation for all you will gain,
Stacey Rose, Ed.S.
Mission Academy Founder

Acknowledgments

My wife is fond of the saying, "It takes a village to raise a child," and I would say the same when writing a book. Or at least influencing a book. My wonderful wife, Anna, needs to be recognized first. Though this book is aimed at helping the church, her heart is more pastorally inclined than mine. Her acknowledgment and encouragement that what I offer in this book is helpful was foundational in my confidence with this project. With her grace, Anna has also helped me become more sensitive to the trusting and leading of the Holy Spirit. Without that influence, I doubt I would have come this far.

My boss, Stacey, also deserves heaps of recognition. She allowed me to live out my calling, to teach the church. Her encouragement and confidence in my abilities are somewhat mystifying, but I've grown so much as an educator and a minister because of her. I would also like to thank her husband, George, who leads a Bible study that keeps me grounded, human, and laughing!

Speaking of those two, they unwittingly took part in a time I half-jokingly call "the summer of wonder," where God did many obvious things in my life to get this book going. Stacey and George introduced me to a beautiful community whose mission is to strengthen and equip laypeople in the church. However, Stacey and George could not have introduced my wife and I to that community if it were not for the McLuhan and Das family, who introduced it to them. So, I'm also in their debt, especially Derryck McLuhan's counsel that it is okay and even good for some Christians to think outside the accepted box.

Acknowledgments

I'd also like to thank Matthew Wimer of Wipf & Stock for taking a chance on me and this book. He doesn't know, but when he reached out with a publication offer, my mother had passed away the previous month, and so, this has all been a soothing balm to my once wearied soul. In this regard, I should also thank Noel, who offered to be a surrogate Dad. He's probably the kindest man I know.

I want to thank all those who've helped to create a deep longing to know the God who is revealed in Jesus Christ and how Scripture points to him. This starts with my parents, who are no longer with us in the body but gave me the gift of growing up in the church. They also introduced me to Gregory A. Boyd as a teen when we started attending Woodland Hills Church, who's been a significant theological influence in my life. My parents also introduced me to writers like C. S. Lewis and J. R. R. Tolkien as a child, and the two authors have come roaring back into my present life. In fact, the resurgence of Lewis's influence probably came from Dr. Tony Richie (featured in this book) when I took his course on the author in seminary. Dr. Richie has been a blessing in my life even after I graduated. He is consistently encouraging and has talked me off a cliff or two. When I expressed my issues with Pentecostalism in his classes, he was gracious but challenged my assumptions, gently forcing me to think more deeply. That, to me, is a sign of a great teacher.

Special thanks to my colleagues at Mission Academy, who've been with me on this journey, especially Sam, who helped me become a better writer. Dr. Jenna Canillas deserves my heartfelt thanks for always believing in me and telling me I'll write many books. My friend Tim, whose question poses a pivotal point of discussion in this book, also warrants praise. Our conversations about Scripture and faith have been formational in ways I didn't realize until I started writing this book.

I wish to recognize my blessed children and my students. If they choose to read this someday, I hope it offers them what they need. Lord knows I needed them. Lastly, how could I not acknowledge our Triune God? May this book bring much glory to God.

Scripture Abbreviations

HEBREW BIBLE/OLD TESTAMENT

Gen	Judg	Neh	Song	Hos	Nah		
Exod	Ruth	Esth	Isa	Joel	Hab		
Lev	1–2 Sam		Job	Jer	Amos	Zeph	
Num	1–2 Kgs		Ps (*pl.* Pss)		Lam	Obad	Hag
Deut	1–2 Chr		Prov	Ezek	Jonah	Zech	
Josh	Ezra	Eccl (or Qoh)		Dan	Mic	Mal	

NEW TESTAMENT

Matt	Acts	Eph	1–2 Tim		Heb	1–2–3 John
Mark	Rom	Phil	Titus	Jas	Jude	
Luke	1–2 Cor		Col	Phlm	1–2 Pet	Rev
John	Gal	1–2 Thess				

OTHER ANCIENT SOURCES

CSEL   *Corpus Scriptorum Ecclesiaticorum Latinorum*

Introduction

WHAT DO YOU THINK of when you hear the word Bible? Do you think of flamboyant televangelists? Do politicians courting a voting block primarily come to mind? Do images of well-meaning aunts who post "biblical warnings" on social media that accompany horrendous art dance through your brain? Or maybe it's not so much those things, but you're a new convert to Christ making your first journey into reading, and you're nervous because you won't understand everything right away? You could be put off by the time commitment it takes to read Scripture. If it isn't that, is it that you've been reading the Bible, but there are a lot of loud voices in our hyper-online world casting doubt on its authenticity and relevancy? Maybe you've been turned off by the vehement arguments of fundamentalists and progressives? If any of those things resonate, this book is for you. Although, this book is also for everyone.

The truth is, there are a lot of loud voices out there, articulate and loud, who do have opinions on what the Bible is, how you should read it, and its relevancy. Because we spend a lot of time online, things like algorithms expose us to these loud, articulate voices, some who have no trouble telling us what we want to hear and who have no issue affirming our doubts, all for visibility and profit.

What are the quiet people saying, though? By nature, I am a quiet person, but if you were to ask me what I thought about the Bible and what in the world God does with it, I would love to share my thoughts with you. That is, essentially, what this book is;

Introduction

the things that I have thought quietly over the past fifteen years of studying Scripture personally and academically.

As to why I've written this book, I know of a few instances in which authors have been inspired to write. Most famously, Tolkien was inspired to write his myths about *The Silmarillion*, *The Hobbit*, and *The Lord of the Rings* because he studied languages and had created his own. For me, though, the inspiration came right in the middle of trying to explain a concept in front of thirty-six or so strangers at a Christian men's retreat. I thought, "Hmm, this would probably make for a helpful book," and the Lord agreed, or perhaps I agreed with him. So, when I returned home from the retreat, I set to begin work on what is now this book.

Another main reason this book exists is simply because of what the subtitle says, to grow your confidence in reading the Bible. That being said, this is not a Christian self-help book; it is not *8 Ways to Increase Your Bible Knowledge Now!* In my view, those types of books don't do much to help a person's faith grow because they promote growth as an instantaneous thing rather than a process that needs to be cultivated. Therefore, let's reject such writings. I also don't offer a way to systematically read the Bible, even if I relied on some commentaries and works of systematic theology while writing. It only occurred to me later that this book is more about how we think about the Bible, and really, how and what we believe about the Bible can determine how and what we think about God. So, with this book, even if it's somewhat short, I want to offer you things you can chew on, mull over, and come to your own conclusions. When we give into such a process, we become more firmly rooted in the life of God.

Although I didn't segment this book into parts, it could be said that the first four chapters provide a pathway for the firm rooting of Scripture to take place in a person's life. What I mean is that I offer ways to help people think about reading the Bible and provide thoughts on what God is doing when we sit down to read it earnestly. For example, this book's opening chapter asks the reader to establish a slower and more meaningful process of reading the Bible. In it, I focus on the importance of meditating on

INTRODUCTION

Scripture while framing the practice in a biblical view and showcasing its benefits for the practical application of Bible reading to our lives. That means defining what meditation is in Christianity and what it isn't.

In chapter two, I contend that Bible reading isn't a single-sided process but one in which God is also involved. The reason for that is not because there isn't any literature out there talking about it, but because it was genuinely life-changing when I came to understand it, so I want to pass on my joy to others. To accomplish this goal, I attempt to guide us through how Scripture supports the Holy Spirit's aid in understanding the biblical text for the believer and how prayer can aid the process.

Suppose we accept that God is involved when an individual and the body of Christ are reading Scripture. In that case, it should open up the idea of acknowledging a supernatural strangeness when wrapping our minds around what's happening in the Bible. Chapter three then examines that type of strangeness and how defining human imagination can help us connect with the strange things written within Scripture. Hopefully, this will guard against any attempts of over-rationalizing, over-reasoning, and over-allegorizing every weird thing away.

When we stop reasoning everything away as if it's swamp gas reflecting the light of the planet Venus, we open ourselves to the fullness of what God is doing in the Bible and through its reading. Chapter four explores the idea of fullness in Scripture and introduces the first of three successive short stories. This chapter's story is aimed at helping us think more deeply about the Bible itself, its themes, and its events in terms of a relationship. For we can't grow in relationships if we only understand a person in a "plain sense." So, we should also determine to understand Scripture beyond a "plain meaning" to approach a fuller relationship with God.

God uses Scripture to disrupt and even shock our sensibilities when we get beyond plain meanings and readings. Chapter five looks at God disrupting our notions by closely examining how redemption is portrayed in the Bible, specifically in the New Testament, and how it contrasts with popular notions of redemption. It,

INTRODUCTION

too, provides another short story to help us consider more deeply how disturbing biblical redemption can be.

Chapter six is sort of a spiritual sequel to the second chapter. It begins with a short story about how a diverse yet united people can turn against each other. Additionally, instead of solely narrowing in on the Spirit himself and his direct illumination of Scripture, I found it essential to widen the scope and highlight how the Spirit works within the global body of the church in terms of understanding Scripture. This is because of the Scriptural importance of seeing the body of Christ as a community and how different parts may have a helpful perspective on Scripture we may not have considered before.

We cannot discuss Scripture without acknowledging Christ because he is the Ultimate Word, whereas the Bible is the penultimate. Chapter seven, then, focuses strictly on Jesus and two specific things the Bible says Jesus is and what those mean for humanity. Incidentally, it's also the longest chapter and, in my opinion, the most important to understand in terms of our identity in him and union with him.

Lastly, chapter eight deals with the writings in the New Testament beyond the gospels. For the willfully ignorant, the New Testament's epistles, or letters, are accused of distorting Jesus' teachings. Instead, the chapter demonstrates how the moral and ethical teachings within them are essential for the continuing work of salvation, which we call sanctification, in the lives of believers.

1

A Storm of Perfection

Concepts create idols; only wonder comprehends anything. People kill one another over idols. Wonder makes us fall to our knees.

—Saint Gregory of Nyssa

Growing up in Minnesota, experiencing thunderstorms was common. I can genuinely say that I enjoyed most of them for one reason or another. Sometimes, when I tell that to others, they give me a strange look, but I never let it bother me. As a child, I particularly enjoyed the storms I could see far in the distance. One of the cool things about living on the northern plains is that the land is level enough so that a person can see storms that are miles away. For whatever reason, my parents told me the lightning we could see from those storms in the distance was called "heat lightning," which never entirely made sense to me but added to their mystique. Those storms always seemed to strike at dusk and in the deepest part of summer. There was just enough light left in the sky that when lightning illuminated the cloud, it took on a curious orangish-white marbled quality that clashed with the deeper blue parts of the thunderhead. Gazing upon those storms in the distance was like looking into a different world; it was great for inspiring the imagination.

The Garden of Scripture

The thunderstorms I usually preferred, however, were the ones that directly impacted us, especially the ones that hit at night. They were never dull. In these storms, one of the main things I enjoyed was how one bolt could light up the surrounding darkness. For the briefest instant, when the lightning struck, I could see every detail of my neighborhood almost as clearly as in the day.

Those childhood memories got put on the back burner. As I moved across the country to the East Coast, thunderstorms were less frequent, and my attention turned to creating and facing my own inner storms. Eventually, I would give my life over to Christ, get married, move to the Southeastern United States, get called into ministry, and go to college and seminary to study theology. With my arrival in the South came the return of natural thunderstorms, ones that, if I can be honest, are terrifying because cloud-to-ground lightning is more common. And trees are everywhere, frequently knocked down by heavy rain and bursts of wind. But they did bring back the memories of watching the lightning illuminate everything.

Then God did something that would make storms relevant in a way I never imagined; he showed me Psalm 119:105. The verse says, "Your word is a lamp to my feet and a light to my path." When I say that God showed it to me, I'm not saying I wasn't aware of the verse; it was a popular worship song when I was a kid and was commonly used as a memory verse in Sunday school. What I mean is that God illuminated it when I studied it in Hebrew. The word for light in Hebrew, *Or*, can mean lightning. Finding that out immediately brought me back to my childhood memory of seeing my surroundings lit up. It revealed to me that the light God provides through his word doesn't just allow us to see a few steps before us but can illuminate our path almost entirely.

As good as that is, lightning is only temporary. Its clarity lasts for a second, and everything goes dark again. When it comes to the direction our lives should go, the major decisions we make, or even the everyday situations we face, we can make the case that we need this type of illumination from God, however brief it is. If we return to Psalm 119:105, God has much more light to give us. *Or*

A Storm of Perfection

does not just mean the brightness that a flash of lightning offers. The word also denotes the light at daybreak, the full light of the sun, and the light of glory, and is even linked to the pillar of fire that Israelites followed coming out of Egypt.

The imagery of lightning and fire almost seems counterintuitive because they are destructive forces, but God is Lord over them and can use those powerful elements. Yahweh himself appeared to the Israelites as a terrifying dark cloud containing lightning and fire. In his ominous interaction with Israel, however, God gave them his *Instruction*, the Torah, that showed Israel how to love and honor him and each other's lives (Exod 19:16–20:17), and that's why *Or* also means the light of life. The overall lesson from Psalm 119:105 is that the light God provides through Scripture is supposed to be stable and consistently shining, leading to a life of love, joy, and eagerness.[1]

Little things like the Hebrew word for light demonstrate how God's Word is perfect. In Evangelical Christianity, we have a strange relationship with that sentiment. By expressing that the Bible is perfect, we usually mean that it is without error and sum it up with a doctrine called Biblical Inerrancy. But that is such a limited view of perfection for Scripture. The Old and New Testaments are perfect not because they don't make errors but because they are the perfect collection of books that speak to humanity's need for salvation. Then it is perfect for speaking to every situation we face because it speaks to the root issues of what causes those situations, doesn't offer a solution found in ourselves, and mainly because it reveals Christ. The little word *Or* implies that our light and lives are sourced and sustained by a perfect God.

MEDITATIVE READING

Our perfect God is willing to give us as much light on his Word as we are eager to ask for, and we should ask. Sometimes, though, I think God nudges us in unexpected ways. He gives us seemingly

---

1. Kraus, *Theology of the Psalms*, 161–162.

perfect moments to reflect on. These perfect moments are typically not easy to define until an individual experiences them, and they are subjective. Perhaps your moment is hearing the first cry of your just-born child or the moment your spouse said "I do" at the altar, or maybe when you realized what you wanted to do for the rest of your life. Whatever those moments are, whenever they do happen, they are engrained in your memory forever.

My moment occurred with my family in the car as we traveled to work and school in the middle of a severe thunderstorm. There was a stretch of road we traveled every day, culminating at a four-way stop. While the drive is ordinarily pleasant because of the surrounding scenery, something more beautiful happened. A strange, otherworldly anxiety, not of impending calamity, but one filled with what I can only describe as awe-filled, began to build in me. The deep-dark color of the sky, the sound of the pounding rain, the lightning, the large trees that lined the sidewalk, and the light from the headlights of cars and small buildings all collided into one of the most beautiful scenes that ever graced my eyes. The moment seemed to freeze in time, and I can only describe it as perfect. And it enchanted my socks off! I've wondered if God was trying to communicate something through what I saw. The only thing I could think of at the time was that he could see me and wanted me to know it. Whatever the case is, it haunts me, and if I am being honest, I want it to haunt me for the rest of my life.

In an important way, I believe the practice of meditating on Scripture can be described as a haunting of God's Word that won't let you go until you spend time with it. Or, at least, maybe that's how we should treat it. When I was a child in the 1980s and '90s, the word meditation certainly would have had a similar connotation with haunting because of its affiliation with Eastern spirituality and New Age practices. However, I have seen the Christian form of meditation become more widely accepted in churches that honor it as a practice within the historical church. But with us having built a society where instant gratification can be met on demand, I wonder if meditation is lacking in the lives of many believers. With so many ways to distract ourselves to prevent us from reflecting, is it any wonder that biblical literacy has significantly declined? Whenever it's done well, however, meditating on Scripture leads to powerful insights that we read about in some of our favorite classic Christian books, such as *The Knowledge of the Holy* by A. W. Tozer. In *Celebration of Discipline*, Richard Foster describes the practice of meditation as the "ability to hear God's voice and obey his word" out of a desire to fellowship with God.[2] Foster pulls from the Bible to note the importance of meditating on Scripture by highlighting the word's use in Psalm 119, where David declares, "Oh, how I love your law! It is my meditation all day long" (119:97) along with other Old Testament appearances.[3] In meditating on God's Word, David found his wisdom had increased significantly and that he could sense his Lord's sweetness, which we don't often take the time to comprehend (119:103). This mirrors the church father Jerome's account of his friend Marcella saying, "whatever in us was gathered by long study and by lengthy meditation was almost changed into nature; this she tasted, this she learned, this she possessed."[4] As a result, when Jerome left his station, Marcella was sought as an authority when issues of Scriptural interpretation arose.[5] So, in a biblical context, meditation doesn't require us to empty our minds or detach ourselves from reality, but it invites us to fill our minds with God's truth to attach ourselves more deeply to him.[6]

Something palpable happens to us after we begin meditating on God's Word; Scripture starts to haunt us. Theologian and educator Cheryl Bridges Johns laments that in this modern age, Scripture doesn't keep people up at night, nor does it seem to fill their

---

2. Foster, *Celebrations of Discipline*, 21. Foster dedicates a whole chapter to the discipline of meditation and deftly cites Scripture to support its use in the Christian life while dispelling misconceptions of the practice.

3. Foster, *Celebrations of Discipline*, 20.

4. Jerome, *Epistle 108*, CSEL 55.334, as quoted in Hall, *Scripture with the Church Fathers*, 44-45.

5. Jerome, *Epistle 108*.

6. Foster, *Celebrations of Discipline*, 25.

days with "images and stories."[7] To cope with that, Johns notices that modern society, Christian or secular, has found alternatives to enchant themselves through popular media or activities driven by lust and has become disenchanted with Scripture. And so, instead, we let a plethora of other harmful things haunt us. With my whole breath, however, I would argue that what the Bible offers us, especially in the revelation of Christ, is beautiful beyond comprehension. We should let such beauty haunt us instead of pain and regret, and it is a shame when we consider the latter more real and tangible than the inhabiting of the Spirit and Word within us. I believe, however, that intentional (which is just a buzzword that means to do something on purpose) meditation is one way to alleviate the issues Johns raises.

Going back to the scene that haunts me, I truthfully am not sure why I had the reaction that I did. It could have been a beautiful sight, not something God was using, except that it led up to a weekend that produced a fantastic amount of freedom in me. Perhaps the Almighty showed me that he can work through anything to show us his glory, and he knows how much I desire to glorify him. So, in meditating on the moment that I experienced, I realized that God used different ingredients to create a masterpiece, or at least to help me see his masterpiece that *is* creation. I then realized that Scripture can be understood in the same way.

But what do I mean by that? Out of contemplation will hopefully come the understanding that Scripture is multifaceted. Each line of Scripture tends to link to other portions of Scripture, forming a connective tissue we banally call themes. If we begin to comprehend specific themes, things like the nature of God's love, faith, the beauty and glory of God's Kingdom, other biblical riches begin to accurately take shape in our hearts and minds. Although the Apostle Paul promises us we'll see through a mirror darkly until Christ's return (1 Cor 13:12), the picture God is communicating to readers of Scripture can become more apparent in meditation.

When the Bible's messages become visible, it's easier to become swept up in its narrative. That is a good thing and arguably what

---

7. Johns, *Re-Enchanting The Text*, 3.

A Storm of Perfection

God wants. A common belief among Christians in the West is that we must interpret God's Word objectively so that we don't insert our own experience into the text; that would be something called eisegesis. However, the unintentional effect of objectivism is that faith becomes an intellectual ascent rather than one that permeates a person's whole self. That is a problem since God is after a person's entire being. Consider Moses' command to the Israelites, saying, "You shall love the Lord your God with all your heart and with all your soul and with all your might" (Deut 6:5), a command that Jesus echoes in Matthew 22. A question we can ask is, if we believe the God revealed in the Bible is powerful enough to create the universe, is he powerful enough to transform us through reading his Word?

Several significant figures throughout the Bible suggest the answer to the question we just asked is yes. One prominent person is the Old Testament leader Joshua. Guess how Joshua says transformation through the Word should happen? He says, "This book of the law shall not depart out of your mouth; you shall *meditate* on it day and night," and in doing so, it will allow us to act in accordance with what it says (Josh 1:8). We must also remember the context of Joshua to understand the significance of how meditating on Scripture can impact the whole person. Joshua had inherited from Moses the role of leading Israel into the promised land of Canaan. He led the Israelites in battle after battle against kingdoms who thought it was perfectly fine to sacrifice children to their gods to receive a fertile growing season. We know this because Moses gives commands to the Israelites, saying:

> When you come into the land that the LORD your God is giving you, you must not learn to imitate the abhorrent practices of those nations. No one shall be found among you who makes a son or daughter pass through fire, or who practices divination, or is a soothsayer, or an augur, or a sorcerer, or one who casts spells, or who consults ghosts or spirits, or who seeks oracles from the dead. For whoever does these things is abhorrent to the LORD; it is because of such abhorrent practices that the LORD your God is driving them out before you. (Deuteronomy 18:9–12)

The kind of thinking and practice of those pagan nations is symbolic of a fallen world. To change such a way of living, the Israelites weren't just required to "know the rules" but to embody the Word of God, which would lead to their prosperity and even the prosperity of their neighbors. It's not so different for Christians in this day and age. Despite Christ inaugurating his Kingdom, we still live in a fallen world and have societies steeped in destructive sin. If meditation could significantly aid the ancient Israelites, we who serve the same God can also benefit.

Although meditation has a profoundly spiritual connotation, many can be turned off by the word or become intimidated. There was and is a long tradition of meditation within the church, often called Contemplative Christianity, a term that can sometimes be code for Christian Mysticism. Like meditation, mysticism can be a polarizing word in some parts of the church because there are other forms of mysticism in different cultures and religions, such as Buddhism and Hinduism. Historically, the church has been enriched by Christian mystics such as Gregory of Nyssa, Augustine, The Desert Fathers (St. Anthony) and Mothers, Hildegard of Bingen, Julian of Norwich, John of the Cross, and many others. Most of the men and women listed lived a monastic life. They dedicated themselves to Christian meditation and other Christian disciplines because it allowed them to be fully devoted to God. Their writings have catapulted them into legendary status with lasting influence.

Yet, if Tim, a close friend of mine who owns a landscaping business, does it while mowing a yard, surely we don't all have to be monks and nuns at a monastery. For Tim, meditation is about asking the Holy Spirit questions about Scripture; a fantastic one that he returns to often is the question of "what happened on the cross?" One could argue that Tim's question is answered directly in the pages of the four gospels. That is true, but meditation is less about seeing what's on the pages and more about dwelling on what the pages reveal, so it's what happens after we see it. That is because the "central goal of Christian mysticism is to experience the ineffable splendors of the mutual indwelling of the soul in Christ,"

A Storm of Perfection

as implied by the Apostle Paul in Ephesians 1:20.[8] The Spirit who inspired the living word invites us to seek with our own spirits the depth of God's communion with us.

We don't have to be monks, priests, pastors, or Apostles to participate in such a communion; we need the willingness to hear God. We will know we've listened to God when we've become more obedient to him and find ourselves growing in the fruit of the Spirit. In his book on the spiritual disciplines, though, Foster laments that people always expect others to speak to God for them as if they prefer to have secondhand knowledge of him.[9] Returning to the story of Yahweh speaking from the mountain in fire, smoke, and lightning, we find that we're not all dissimilar from the Israelites who requested a mediator between themselves and Yahweh because they thought they'd die (Deut 5:22–27). But we serve a God who wants us to have life and have it abundantly (John 10:10b). The only mediator we need is Christ Jesus, and he happens to be God who reigns in our hearts and asks us to abide in him (John 15:4–10).

Also, consider this: the Hebrew word for meditate, *hagita*, means "to mutter" or to "say under the breath," which brings a kind of lightness to the practice. There is a reason for muttering. Since most Israelites learned God's Word orally, it only makes sense that lingering on it would also be verbal itself. So, those who meditated on the Law would walk around or perform their duties while muttering Scripture under their breath in the process of understanding. Lots of us mutter under our breath, and usually, it's by saying something passive-aggressive. Imagine, though, if we instead directed our thoughts and words towards understanding a verse or a passage we long to comprehend. I believe it would bring significant change to our lives and compel us to do it more and more as we seek to commune with God and obey him.

---

8. McColman, *The Big Book of Christian Mysticism*, 50.
9. Foster, *Celebrations of Discipline*, 28.

THE GARDEN OF SCRIPTURE

HOW TO MEDITATE ON SCRIPTURE AS A CHRISTIAN

So, how does a Christian meditate on their Bible readings? In this section, I'm supposed to offer several tips on how to improve your contemplative life. The fact is that it is difficult to flesh out concretely. The Bible, of course, is primary. Having the verse or passage fresh in our minds helps the process significantly as we seek to ask and dwell on its meaning. Richard Foster, who I mentioned earlier, writes about developing an interior life aided by time, place, and posture.[10] Time is crucial because we have the physical and the emotional competing with the spiritual. The place is significant because it might be impossible to get a moment's peace depending on our environment. Posture also impacts us because we can't think or reflect well if we're uncomfortable.

I agree with Foster. I often meditate on Scripture when I'm alone and have ambient music playing while sitting at my desk with the blinds open so I can see my yard. That being said, I've also meditated when doing the dishes, cutting the grass, or vacuuming. Anything that relies on muscle memory, or a "mindless activity," frees our minds to focus on what we've read and be receptive to the Spirit of God. Notice here, too, in all these instances, as well as what Foster suggests, that I am wide awake. I like to think of meditating as studying in that it's a process of learning, and I'm giving it the kind of attention needed to study well. It's probably not impossible to meditate on Scripture lying in bed, but it's less fruitful because of the temptation to doze off. Additionally, in times of meditation, you may want to write down the verse or passage so that you can come back later and add anything that God has shown you or if any of your other readings have contributed to your understanding.

GETTING RESULTS?

So far, I have described meditation as seeking answers and communing with God. We do this expecting that God will speak to

---

10. Foster, *Celebrations of Discipline*, 31–33.

us in return. But when can we expect an answer or see results? Whenever. I mentioned above that I, and others, have meditated during purposeful times or when doing mindless tasks. God also spoke to me in those times by impressing a thought that directly addressed what I was searching for in meditation. However, God has also spoken to me while I was in the middle of teaching my students. As I was writing *The Fruit That Turns The World Upside Down*, I'd been doing a lot of meditative reading. While teaching my high school students about the flood in Genesis, a thought literally popped into my head about how the flood metaphorically applies to our lives before we meet Christ and how Christ's peace changes the effect of water to sanctify us.[11] I believe I said, "holy smokes," out loud while writing on the marker board. All that to say, I wasn't expecting such a thought at that time.

If our meditation is truly about God, I believe he also gives us a way to confirm it. Countless times after meditation, questions have formed in my mind about God and what he says in his Word, and numerous times, that question was answered via a pastor's sermon or perhaps something another Christian said, and usually in the same week. It is vital to confirm what we're getting from meditation so we don't slip into false beliefs and share erroneous things outside the bounds of Scripture. We need to heed John's words to "not believe every spirit, but test the spirits to see whether they are from God; for many false prophets have gone out into the world" (1 John 4:1). Nevertheless, if we're receptive to God, he will bless us in his timing, which, by our standards, may happen whenever.

We love mysteries, but more than that, we love solving puzzles. One of my favorite mystery-solving television series was *Luther*, starring Idris Elba, because it's not Sherlock Holmes but is still set in London. As a detective, Luther faces off against some very dangerous and brilliant foes, especially Alice Morgan, but he always manages to crack the case. Part of what I love about

---

11. Tschida, *The World Upside Down*, 13–14. In the end of the first chapter, I link God separating the waters of chaos in Genesis 1 to God flooding the world in Genesis 6 because our sin seems to desire chaos, so God gave the chaos they wanted by giving them the flood waters. In this day and age, the chaos caused by sin can flood our lives, and God lets us experience that.

mystery shows is misdirection. When the viewer thinks they've figured out who's done it, the detective reveals who *actually* did the crime, and there is closure. Some people take the same approach when meditating on Scripture as if the rest of the church is getting specific passages wrong, but their meditation reveals what the Bible is *really* saying. We are not Gnostics who try to "unlock" secret truths in the Bible or who eschew our physical lives for a solely spiritual life. While Christian meditation involves a person's mind and spirit, the practice rests in the God present in both Testaments. Through meditation, we embrace the tension of mystery, understanding that God may reveal some parts but not all.

It is like *The Big Bang Theory* episode called "The Closure Alternative." In the episode, one of the main characters, Sheldon Cooper (Jim Parsons), is upset about his favorite show being canceled on a cliffhanger. Sensing his obsession with closure in many other parts of his life and thinking he needs to re-condition his mind, Sheldon's girlfriend, Amy (Mayim Bialik), arranges a series of activities for him to complete but prevents him from completing each task just before he can finish. By the end of the night, Sheldon claims that her experiment worked and confesses, albeit somewhat falsely, that he doesn't need the closure he sought.[12]

There are vast differences, of course. God's story is not a sitcom, and he's not devising things for us and pulling the rug out from under us before we finish. However, God wants us to recondition our minds and form us, and he even wants us to be content with never knowing everything. For example, we may never understand completely the mystery of the Trinity. Yet, through meditation, we may see more and more how the Father, Son, and Holy Spirit interact in Scripture.

Mystery is beneficial for our minds. Why shouldn't we want to let our minds hold God and his love in awe and wonder? Because those two states of being lead to feeling overwhelmed, people often avoid such a crucial time of reflection. As the Norwegian Educator Paul Martin Opdal observes, awe and "Wonder . . . always points

---

12. Lorre, *The Big Bang Theory*.

to something beyond the accepted rules."[13] That can be daunting, especially in the context of religion, where there are "rules" to prevent us from sliding into unorthodox beliefs. Yet, multiple times in Scripture, we are told that being in awe and wonder of God is more than acceptable. Opdal notes that wonder gives us "an inkling that there is more to it that tradition admits, and that this 'more' can be investigated."[14] The "more" can be described as the theology beyond denominational doctrine that can sometimes be too reductive in how it discusses God and what he does.

Therefore, meditation can and does serve as a direct link to awe and wonder. In fact, we could say that meditation allows us to dive into the depths, swim in the mysteries Scripture presents, and enjoy that God is wholly other than us and who makes us whole.

WHAT MEDITATION ON SCRIPTURE ISN'T

The spiritual practice of Christian meditation is not a trend either. Trends depend on the consensus of popularity and are driven by influencers. For example, at the time of this writing, it is 2023, and a famous haircut from the early 1990s, the mullet, is gaining popularity because of some musicians and professional athletes. God willing, the trend will die out again, too. Although Christian spiritual practices have ebbed and flowed within the church for the last two thousand years, and some believers have promoted spirituality for their own benefit, practices such as meditation are a core component of the faith. As I have already demonstrated, meditation has been part of biblical faith since its inception, with its first appearance in Genesis 24:63. For Christians, intentional practice within the church was emphasized in the patristic period, if not before. Christopher Hall writes:

> The [church] fathers never split theology off from spirituality, as though theology was an academic, mental exercise best practiced in one's study, while Christian

---

13. Opdal, "Curiosity, Wonder, and Education," 331.
14. Opdal, "Curiosity, Wonder, and Education," 331.

spirituality was more appropriately focused on the heart and centered in a church sanctuary. Any split between mind and heart, theology and spirituality, study and sanctuary would have been met with scant toleration from the fathers.[15]

Deitrich Bonhoeffer utilized meditation as well. A commonly shared quote from him states, "Why do I meditate? Because I am a Christian."[16] That is because Bonhoeffer believed it to be an excellent way to tame the flesh, the fallen nature that tries daily to creep up in believers and distracts us from forming good Christian discipleship.[17] He knew that our spirits are all too willing to follow the path of discipleship, but the flesh is "fearful," causing us to create distractions and excuses as to why we can't grow in our love toward God and our neighbor.[18] Carving out time for meditating on Scripture is a practical discipline for our faith as we humbly submit ourselves to "move forward with certainty upon the firm ground of the word of God."[19]

Lastly, meditation is not for our self-elevation and self-promotion. Social media can sometimes be a great place for Christians. Through it, I've gained a lot of relationships with people that wouldn't be possible without the platforms. On the other hand, social media is also rife with temptation, which includes the temptation to appear more pious than everyone else. With the surge of re-discovering the patristic and medieval period of Christianity in Evangelicalism, one of my worries is that some believers would co-opt the spiritual practices and theology of the church fathers and lord it over others who were less informed or use their spiritual practices to skirt moral and ethical issues Scripture warns against. We do not have to look too far to see examples. However, the flaunting of Christian spirituality and its misappropriation makes it void. Meditation done well should drive our pretensions away

---

15. Hall, *Theology With The Church Fathers*, 10
16. Bonhoeffer, *Meditating On The Word*, 22.
17. Bonhoeffer, *Discipleship*, 159.
18. Bonhoeffer, *Discipleship*, 159.
19. Bonhoeffer, *Meditating on the Word*, 22.

rather than enable them. Therefore, the more we meditate on the Word, the more it can be mapped over our lives since the practice's goal is the application of Scripture. In short, meditation helps us decrease as Christ increases.

2

Prayer and the Spirit

God knows absolutely the thoughts of all. What the voice communicates to us, our thoughts speak to God.

—Clement of Alexandria

I WENT TO COLLEGE a total of three times. Once, I went to a community college when I lived in Massachusetts, another time to a state university here in Georgia, and finally, to Lee University, where I graduated. At each institution, I tried my hand at developing my writing. At first, it was mainly fiction, but when I attended the state university, I was required to take a college composition course that was disastrous and very defeating to someone in their late twenties. Worse, when I sought guidance from the professor about switching to a lower-level class to develop my skills, he told me he couldn't advise me and that the decision was up to me. It was very distressing that he was more than willing to let me know what was wrong with my writing but wouldn't instruct and advise me on how to improve it. I ultimately dropped that class and had to take an academic penalty.

A few years later, during my first semester at Lee, I was forced to take a similar composition course. My professor, however, took a completely different approach. Instead of being distant and uncaring, she was insightful and encouraging. She was the one to help me know what kind of writer I am, having a voice and a style that mirrored other writers who'd contributed great things to the world. It's more than that; Professor Yaun *wanted* me to understand.

Now, I'm the teacher. My students range from second grade to high school unless it's Friday chapel, where I teach all grades. My responsibility is to guide them in all things history and Bible, which is a huge responsibility. One of my duties is getting them comfortable using a Bible. Usually, even if they have a background in the church, my invitation to go and get a Bible off the shelf is met with a groan or wide-eyed terror. For the ones who groan, I can only assume that Bible reading is done for them, and they don't want the extra work, or they just might not be invested. However, most of the latter have never handled a Bible or attempted to read it and are intimidated by its length and the non-modern way Scripture communicates.

With both sets of students, though, my approach and attitude about Bible reading and their ability to understand it matters most. If a student is a new reader of God's Word and can't locate the passage I ask them to find and I get frustrated with them, it can likely harm their confidence in navigating Scripture. If I mock their inability to interpret a verse they've never seen before but I have read a multitude of times, it will most likely make them wonder if they should pick it back up again. No, I *want* my students to understand what they're reading, and I *want* them to know they can be good readers of the Bible and apply it to their lives at their age. So, building their confidence is critical because the better they understand, the more truthful their knowledge of God will be.

It is the same for adults. Although I can't say for sure that many are intimidated by reading the Bible, I am willing to bet there are plenty of people who are, and it may be for the same reason my students are scared. Nevertheless, our God is relational, and though he has complete knowledge of us and our hearts, he also desires us to have knowledge of his heart. But again, this is not just intellectual knowledge we're accustomed to today. No, to be relational means to be multi-dimensional. This is why the Hebrew word *yada* is one of my favorite words. It means "to know" and touches on the intellectual/cognitive sense but is also used in the emotional and experiential senses of knowing (more on this in chapter 7).[1] For example, the Egyptians came to know Yahweh was leading the Israelites because all the plagues they experienced could only come from him (Exod 7:5). The penitent woman washes the feet of Jesus with her tears, which are a result of emotions because of what he's done for her (Luke 7:38). So, again, like with meditation, the whole of a person is involved when it comes to having knowledge of God.

We can come to this type of holistic knowledge not just through reading the Bible but with what the Holy Spirit does through us reading it. Being what we call the third person of the Trinity, the Holy Spirit is God and has demonstrated his activity in many ways, as the Bible shows. One of the main ways he works is to *reveal* the Word of God. When we see the Spirit of God mentioned, we know that God is about to do something big. We can see this by going all the way back to the first few sentences of Genesis, "Now the earth was formless and empty, darkness covered the surface of the watery depths, and *the Spirit of God* was hovering over the surface of the waters" (Gen 1:2 CSB, emphasis mine). In the following sentence, God speaks the first light of creation into existence. In this case, the Holy Spirit anticipates God's authoritative and creative words that usher in creation and bring order out of chaos.

When humanity messed things up and created the world's first blame game in Eden, however, God remained relational and endowed certain people, both men and women, with his Spirit, who had the authority to speak on his behalf (Num 11:17, Ezek 2:2, Mic 3:5), a group of men and women called the prophets. The Israelites often found these people were actual prophets of God because these empowered men and women never affirmed how Israel wanted to live. They called for holiness to God and faithfulness to the covenant, which was inconvenient because it interfered with greed and earthly delights. When real prophets were allowed to

---

1. Martens, *God's Design*, 92–93.

speak in some royal courts, the kings complained these people of God "never had anything good to say" (1 Kgs 22:8). Nevertheless, what God spoke through the Spirit-empowered prophets always came to pass. Depending on Israel's response, it was sometimes a blessing and sometimes a disaster.

On the other hand, there is freedom where the Spirit of the Lord is. Could you imagine what would have happened if the Israelites had heeded the words of the prophets the Spirit of God spoke through them? Remember, the Spirit was active in the creation of the universe. In many instances, the Hebrew word used for spirit, *ruach*, also means wind and breath. The Old Testament scholar John Goldingay tells us that wind is dynamic because it is invisible yet powerful, as those who've faced a hurricane would know. So, the wind symbolizes God unleashing his divine power into the world.[2] For something to have breath, as we all know, means that it also has life. We are reminded that God breathed the breath of life into Adam. Hearing and obeying the Word of God through the prophets was a chance to experience the life and power of God, which ultimately would have brought them freedom. Despite sporadic periods of faithfulness, Israel would ultimately reject that freedom and the cost was being exiled to a foreign nation.

But God was not done. Four hundred years or so later, after Jews began returning from exile, the gospel of Luke tells us that the Holy Spirit conceived a child in Mary, a descendant of King David (Luke 1:35), who would be the long-awaited Messiah of Israel, Jesus. When Mary visits her cousin Elizabeth, who had miraculously conceived a child in her old age several months earlier, Luke says, "the baby leaped inside her, and Elizabeth was filled with the Holy Spirit" (1:41). This is essential. As many may know, Elizabeth's child was John the Baptist, whose preaching of repentance, following Israel's prophetic tradition and therefore considered God's Word, would be responsible for helping people's hearts to receive the ministry of Christ Jesus.

John's gospel shifts the paradigm for us and probably for many in Christ's day of how the Word of God is understood. It

---

2. Goldingay, "The Breath of Yahweh," 4.

could be said we understand the Word of God as referring to the Torah, which many called the Law, and it also meant the ministry of the prophets who God spoke through and were eventually written down. This is what is called the inscripturated Word of God. In John, however, we learn that the Word was made flesh in Jesus, meaning he is the incarnated Word of God (John 1:14).[3] The Holy Spirit continued his work after conceiving Christ, the Incarnated Word. He also anointed Jesus during his baptism in the river Jordan, painting a beautiful Trinitarian picture of God, including the Father acknowledging Jesus as his Son (Luke 3:21–22). Soon after, through the power of the Spirit, Jesus would victoriously use the inscripturated Word to defeat the temptation attempts of Satan and then declare in the synagogue of Nazareth that he was the fulfillment of Isaiah's messianic prophecy (Luke 4:1–21).

Like many prophets before him, Jesus paid the price for his ministry with his life by the very people he was sent to serve. However, those of us who've read the gospel accounts have the benefit of knowing that Jesus wasn't just a Spirit-endowed prophet; he's the Messiah. But he's also the Word who was with God in the beginning and the Word who *is* God, and so while he entered into death, it couldn't ultimately hold him. This was the Spirit and the Word working together again. The Spirit raised Jesus from the dead, and the Word of God was lifted back to the world and then to the Father (Rom 8:11).

And they weren't done yet. Before ascending into the heavens, Jesus tells his disciples to wait for the Holy Spirit to appear in Jerusalem. He did. In an event that mirrored the wind, smoke, and fire of Mount Sinai, in the book of Exodus, the Holy Spirit blew in like a mighty wind and anointed those gathered with tongues of fire. This time, they didn't display the same kind of fear the Israelites had, and through their submission to what the Spirit was doing, Babel was reversed as men and women passing by heard their own languages being spoken. The Word became for

---

3. Hereafter incarnated will be Incarnated to represent the historic Christian doctrine.

all nations,[4] just as the prophets of old had preached through their Spirit-inspired proclamations. The first churches were born, and many people in different lands came to hear the Incarnate Word (Jesus) being proclaimed.

The Holy Spirit, then, prepared for and revealed the oral/written word of God and the Incarnate Word of God, Jesus. In each instance, God eagerly invites his people to come to the knowledge of himself, first through the Torah and the prophets and then through the Son (Heb 1:1-2). Even though we're redeemed, however, Christians are not infallible. We are prone to a short memory and still face a world being tossed around in waves of confusion, and these realities show up when we attempt to read our Bibles.

Jesus was prepared for that before we picked up our Bibles. There were men and women who needed to preach his gospel to religious people who believed they knew God's Word and to people who worshipped many gods. That is why Jesus sent the Holy Spirit as their Advocate (John 14:26). With such opposition and competition, the fledgling community of Christ's followers would need to be reminded of the truth of what was taught to them by Jesus (16:13). So when the Spirit rushed into the upper room, the Apostles weren't just equipped with the power to perform signs and wonders, they were furnished with an abiding truth.

That is a big deal! The fact that the first Christians didn't have to solely rely on their memory means they could continue encountering the risen Jesus because of the Spirit's work.[5] New Testament scholar Craig Koester says the Spirit discloses Jesus as a "living presence" within the church after the first Easter.[6] We see this living presence manifesting in a few different places in Acts, but predominantly with the event of Peter and Cornelius in Acts 9 and 10, where the conversion of Gentiles into Christianity officially kicks off. From there, the majority of Acts focuses on the truth of Christ preached to the nations by Paul, and he would eventually

---

4. The word of God, in the sense of all Scripture, and the Word of God as Jesus.
5. Koester, *The Word of Life*, 150.
6. Koester, *The Word of Life*, 150.

THE GARDEN OF SCRIPTURE

give his life for the fact, as would many other Apostles. Still, Christ was present with them as he is with the rest of his followers, even in this age (Matt 28:20).

SPIRIT-LED READING

The canon of Scripture is closed now, but the world still needs the truth of Christ. Though we have the Bible, believing God expects us to read it without his help would be dangerous. If the Spirit leads us into all truth, and if Jesus, who is the way, the truth, and the life, and whose gospel is contained within God's Word, it is consistent with the character of the Holy Spirit to illuminate what God has revealed in the past and what has been revealed about God through Jesus. What is contained in Scripture is the very heart of God poured out for the salvation of his people. Although we see the words of God printed in the text, they're still things that have been spiritually revealed to the writers of the Old and New Testaments. Therefore, they must also be understood by our heart, mind, soul, and spirit.

 The Apostle Paul speaks to the reality of a holistic understanding of God's revelation in First Corinthians. He tells his hearers/readers that the revelation of Christ was a secret knowledge deep within God (1 Cor 2:7). Only the Holy Spirit knew because just like our own spirits know what's deeply held within us, only God's Spirit can search his own depths (2:10). Christians, however, have received God's Spirit at the moment of salvation so that "we might understand the things freely given us by God" (2:12b, ESV). Paul says the truth preached is spiritual wisdom and needs to be spiritually comprehended rather than just with the natural mind (2:13–14).

 William Barclay helps us better understand what the Apostle Paul teaches in this passage. He notes that Paul distinguishes between two kinds of people, the *pneumatikoi* and the *psuchikos*.[7] The first one shares the Greek word for "spirit," *pneuma*, making

---

7. Barclay, *The Letters to the Corinthians*, 28.

that person sensitive to the Holy Spirit and therefore led by him.[8] The second shares the Greek word for "soul," *psuche*, but it is bound up in humanity, sharing only the nature of physical life with every other living being.[9] The *psuchikos* person lives as if there is nothing other than the present bodily life. This means such a man or woman only values the material and physical; they have no desire to understand the virtues of chastity, generosity, and spirituality. Instead, they will only seek fulfillment in sexual gratification, amassing material wealth and an end in themselves, which, in turn, will lead to spiritual deafness and blindness.[10] The Christ follower, however, is the *pneumatikoi*, who can discern the spiritual and understand Scripture confidently, expecting their understanding to grow over a lifetime with the Spirit's help.

PRAYER AND READING

One of the best ways to become sensitive to the leadership of the Holy Spirit is through prayer. Like Bible reading, however, a good prayer life can be challenging and even seem bothersome depending on the time we are willing to commit to the practice. Insecurities can come into play as well. In his book on how the patristics worshiped, Christopher Hall laments, "The moment I sit down to pray I feel as though ten thousand bumble bees are flying through the atmosphere of my brain."[11] I face my fair share of issues, too. For example, I've never been a great verbal communicator; I have a slight stutter and often trip over my words, so it is difficult to pray out loud when it's just me and God. I have also been in the

---

8. Barclay, *The Letters to the Corinthians*, 28.

9. Barclay, *The Letters to the Corinthians*, 28. Barclay remarks that all humanity has pneuma, but that's what makes it distinct above the rest of creation because other living things do not.

10. Barclay, *The Letters to the Corinthians*, 28. One could argue that Paul was saying that those who chose only to live in terms of "the physical life" and ignoring their spirit are choosing to live like animals since animals are devoid of *pneuma*.

11. Hall, *Worshiping With The Church Fathers*, 63.

company of some wonderful saints who seem to have been bred to pray, and it left me feeling a little inferior. Nevertheless, God is much larger than our defects and makes up for what we lack, so I always find myself talking to God.

Maybe you're like me. Or perhaps you don't know what to pray because so much is overwhelming around you. Possibly, you are like the person Thomas Merton describes as someone who, in prayer, gets in your own way so badly that you become completely paralyzed and can't act like a normal human being.[12] The Spirit, our Helper, and Advocate, wants to help us there; as the Apostle Paul says,

> . . . the Spirit helps us in our weakness; for we do not know how to pray as we ought, but that very Spirit intercedes with sighs too deep for words. And God, who searches the heart, knows what is the mind of the Spirit, because the Spirit intercedes for the saints according to the will of God. (Rom 8:26–27)

However, how can the Spirit intercede for us if we're not bothering to pray? He may still be, but the point further speaks to God's relational nature: to have you know him as your Abba Father.

What happens in prayer is primarily the work of God. But we still have the responsibility to enter into it. The first-century church knew this all too well. From the beginning of the book of Acts to the end of Revelation, prayer and events happening in the context of prayer occur approximately eighty-two times. A handful of those prayers involve understanding God's self-revelation to his people. This can be seen in the first chapter of Ephesians, where Paul lets his readers know how he's praying for them, writing, "I pray that the God of our Lord Jesus Christ, the Father of glory, may give you a spirit of wisdom and revelation as you come to know him, so that, with the eyes of your heart enlightened, you may perceive what is the hope to which he has called you" (Eph 1:17–18b). This echoes a similar prayer he informs the Colossian church, telling them he's praying so that they "may be filled with the knowledge of God's will in all spiritual wisdom and understanding" (Col 1:9b).

---

12. Merton, *No Man Is An Island*, 32.

Prayer and the Spirit

All of this is to say that as we open our Bibles, praying is appropriate and necessary. In fact, beginning with prayer is part of the meditative reading of Scripture. It is the action of humbling ourselves to be instructed by God and his Word and the opportunity to commune on a profoundly personal and spiritual level with him. We do well when we remember that accepting Christ means we're a child of God. We've been adopted into it because Christ reconciled us to God, and His Spirit has been placed in us. Being *the* skilled Creator, our God wants us to understand Him and what He does, and that's why we have Scripture.

On the other hand, He is not the distant landlord of the deists, nor is he the stern, battle-scarred, hot-tempered, and white-haired grandfather the Gnostics saw in the Old Testament. No, our Triune God wants us to communicate with Him in such a fashion that it shapes us. Scripture even says that we can approach his "throne of grace with boldness, so that we may receive mercy and find grace to help in *time of need*" (Heb 4:16, emphasis mine), I would argue that understanding the Bible is necessitated as a time of need.

It is a time of need. What makes reading the Bible such a time is what it does for the believer; it equips our faith. Many Christians are familiar with what the Apostle Paul says to his protégé, Timothy, writing, "All Scripture is inspired by God and is useful for teaching, for reproof, for correction, and for training in righteousness, so that everyone who belongs to God may be proficient, equipped for every good work" (2 Tim 3:16–17). While it's critical to recognize that the words of the Bible were breathed out by God, Paul stresses its usefulness above all.[13] Saying the Bible is useful seems a bit bland and reductionist, but we need to see it through the lens of Paul and the other Apostles' eyes. In the ancient world, what made a doctrine valuable was its ability to transform life, and the Bible is the God-given resource for "discerning and measuring God's self-revelation within human existence."[14] So, yes, the Bible is useful, but in a way that changes us.

---

13. Johnson, *Letters to Timothy*, 420.
14. Johnson, *Letters to Timothy*, 422.

Then there is also the reality of praying the Scriptures. In Evangelical and Pentecostal circles, we certainly pray the Lord's Prayer, which Jesus teaches in Matthew 6:9–13. When we examine the passage closely, as other authors have done, we see that even that pocket-sized prayer communicates how much God wants us to know him. For example, when Jesus instructs in the prayer to ask, "Give us today our daily bread," he calls back to the daily provision of manna God provided the Israelites during their Exodus from Egypt. Therefore, Jesus states that God desires to provide not only our spiritual lives but also our physical lives. Jesus is saying that God is still Jehovah Jireh and that we should always know him that way.

However, in the book *Worshiping With the Church Fathers*, author Christopher Hall reveals to his readers that ancient Christians prayed the Psalms. They did this because "they increasingly realized that by praying the Psalms David's experiences in prayer and spiritual growth could become their own."[15] If we think about it, it makes sense. Even though the words of the Psalms are written by human hands, they are ultimately inspired by the Holy Spirit. Therefore, if the Holy Spirit is working in our prayers to help us understand Scripture, would not the very words inspired by Him be appropriate to pray? I believe so, as do many other Christian traditions who continue to pray the Psalms. However, we should also consider the New Testament prayers since their ultimate author is the same Holy Spirit.

We have seen then that God does not leave us out in the cold when reading his Word. He's been working since the beginning not only to bring us what we now call the Bible but also to help us come to know him through the illuminating work of His Spirit and the vital practice of prayer. I think I'm supposed to say something witty now to close this chapter, but I want you to know and love God as much as I do. It has taken time to get here, and that's a good thing, but I couldn't get here without spending intentional time in the pages of the Bible with prayer and the Spirit helping to guide me.

---

15. Hall, *Worshiping With The Church Fathers*, 68.

3

Embracing The Strange

It is not possible for the mind to crash suddenly past the familiar into the totally unfamiliar.[1]

—A. W. Tozer

THERE ARE A FEW times that I can recall being genuinely scared in my life. When I was a child, I was traumatized by the movie *Ghost* when evil spirits came to drag away the villains to hell. Another time was starting my first job in Massachusetts after having moved there a few months earlier; I had been so paralyzed by anxiety that I almost couldn't get out of bed. Towering over those two instances was when I was sitting in a movie theater in Eugene, Oregon. I had traveled there with my wife and our young daughter to visit friends, one of whom invited me to speak at the church he and his wife pastored at the time. During the movie, so many people were continuously leaving and coming back into the theater, and it seemed to span the entire length of the film. My friend seemed oblivious to all the movement, and he said as much when I mentioned it on the car ride back to his apartment.

1.. Tozer, *Knowledge Of The Holy*, 6.

The Garden of Scripture

It could have been my nerves getting to me. I'd never been to a place like Eugene, a place with unnatural greenness and one of the largest homeless encampments in the United States. The pastor I mentioned told me that the people of Eugene are physically active in terms of their health and social justice. He, in fact, joked that the people would even protest protesting if given a chance. But I could have also been sensing a restless and anxious spirit that inhabited the people in the cinema. Whatever the case, everything was alien to me; I felt like I was on a different planet, and in that movie theater, I was terrified.

At the same time, the fear that I experienced was motivational. It seemed like the city was challenging me to a duel, and I wanted to accept. In the next few days, I had set my sights on moving my wife and our two kids there. Those plans eventually fell apart, and we stayed in Georgia, but I desperately wanted to embrace what was strange even though it scared the daylights out of me.

Maybe some of my students feel that way about reading the Bible. The Bible is, after all, strange, and that's something we should readily admit. Our Triune, transcendent, and imminent God uses Scripture to reveal himself and the plan of salvation to his fallen creations. But those qualities can't be fully communicated by human language or always be easily understood by the human mind. I would also suggest that we are a self-centered race who can't or won't always comprehend the reality that other beings with greater intelligence exist on a spiritual plane. Our "enlightened" minds reserve things like that for fairy stories and science-fiction.

The writers of Scripture make no defense against the strange things they communicate. And they do say weird things. Take, for example, this passage from Ezekiel:

> As I looked at the living creatures, I saw a wheel on the earth beside the living creatures, one for each of the four of them. As for the appearance of the wheels and their construction: their appearance was like the gleaming of beryl; and the four had the same form, their construction being something like a wheel within a wheel. When they

Embracing The Strange

moved; they moved in any of the four directions without veering as they moved. Their rims were tall and awesome, for the rims of all four were full of eyes all around. When the living creatures moved, the wheels moved beside them; and when the living creatures rose from the earth, the wheels rose. Wherever the spirit would go, they went, and the wheels rose along with them; for the spirit of the living creatures was in the wheels. When they moved, the others moved; when they stopped, the others stopped; and when they rose from the earth, the wheels rose along with them; for the spirit of the living creatures was in the wheels. (Ezek 1:15–21)

A new reader might be alarmed that they'd need to make sense of the vision in this passage from Ezekiel with such a description. This chunk of Scripture follows a depiction of the four living creatures' appearances that is just as bizarre, and the vision continues until the end of the chapter.[2] It should be noted that even scholars who study these passages professionally have mixed interpretations of what's happening in this specific passage. But everything the authors of Scripture describe in the Bible is written for a reason; there are no throw-away lines.

A FIRST STEP IN UNDERSTANDING

The images in Scripture that are difficult to picture in the mind and seem unbelievable to us matter greatly. From a sea splitting in two to a city descending from the heavens, God challenges our modern minds with strangeness to have us try and comprehend a reality beyond what we can see. However, the question becomes, how do we accept the peculiar things we read about in the Bible? I will propose an initial step by pointing to one of Jesus' teachings.

In the Gospel of Matthew, Jesus' disciples drum up the courage to ask somewhat of a ludicrous question that Mark's gospel account says they'd been arguing about. The question they posed to

2. Sweeny, *Reading Ezekiel*, 64–65. Sweeny suggests too many get stuck on the specifics of conceptualizing how the wheels should appear in one's mind but argues that the tactic misses the point of what Ezekiel describes.

their master was: "Who is the greatest in the kingdom of heaven" (Matt 18:1)? Instead of scolding them, Jesus used their shortsightedness as another lesson. Matthew goes on to say, "He called a child, whom he put among them, and said, 'Truly I tell you, unless you change and become like children, you will never enter the kingdom of heaven'" (18:2–3).

For our purposes, two things can be gleaned from that passage. The first is that Jesus calls out his disciples' lack of humility by giving them an example of that trait. New Testament scholar N. T. Wright suggests that Jesus called this child to stand among them because children are "vulnerable, unsure of themselves, but trusting with clear eyes, ready to listen, to be loved and to love, to learn and grow."[3] As a teacher of kids from the age of eight up to eighteen, I generally agree with Wright's assessment of a child's characteristics (It takes particular reasons for children to not be like that through the intentional choices of an adult). If we are to be great in God's Kingdom, not only do we need to adopt the humility of a child as we learn from our big brother, Jesus, and what God reveals throughout Scripture, but we need to put that childlike humility into practice.[4]

However, another part of a child's humility that needs to be addressed is the openness of using the imagination. Here, we don't need to go into the discussion of how badly the word "imagination" has been tarnished in both history and religion nor do we need to discuss how a child's imagination works or deal with fictional works of literature and film, we just need to define and discuss why using the imagination as a Christian is essential.

IMAGINATION IN THE BIBLE

In this area, it would be helpful if the word itself appeared in the original languages of the Bible, but it doesn't. The closest we get to the imagination as something literal is when the writers of

---

3. Wright, *Matthew: Part Two*, 28.
4. Wright, *Matthew: Part Two*, 28

Embracing The Strange

Scripture talk about what is devised in a person's head and heart. This matches up with the explanation that imagination is crucial for planning because it "sets out a course of action that is directed at closing the gap between the world as it is conceived to be and as it actually is (possibly more compatible with one's desires)."[5] Unfortunately, most allusions to the human imagination in the Bible are in a negative context. For example, for the people of Noah's day, "every *inclination of the thoughts* of their hearts was only evil continually" (Gen 6:5, emphasis mine). The writer of Proverbs warns against "a heart that *devises* wicked plans, feet that hurry to run to evil" (Prov 16:18, emphasis mine). In his sermon on the mount, Jesus says that any man who looks at a woman with *lustful intent* has already committed adultery (Matt 5:28, emphasis mine).

On the other hand, humans keep imagining. This is a consequence of being created in the image of God. Since he is the Creator, as J. R. R. Tolkien says, "being made by a creator, one of our natural factors is wishing to create,"[6] and therefore, we use our imaginations, which are intrinsically linked to creativity, even if those two are marred by sin. Yet, as Mr. Wisdom says in C. S. Lewis's *The Pilgrims Regress*, the wise man disciplines his imagination.[7] The head and heart of the Christian then are called to be renewed and transformed so that they can reflect a holy character and the mind of Christ (Rom 12:2, Phil 2:5). Therefore, we can say that the Christian imagination is the thoughts of a person's heart and mind that are turned toward God, or as the Apostle Paul says, we are taking "every thought captive to obey Christ" (2 Cor 10:5). It is our communion with God that creates the devising of thoughts that please him.

Similarly, the Bible practically begs its readers to use their imaginations creatively. Indeed, there is no escape from using the

---

5. Reuland, "Imagination, Planning, and Working Memory," S99.
6. BBC Archive, "1962: Tolkien."
7. Lewis, *The Pilgrim's Regress*, 135. Mr. Wisdom says that disciplined imagination *and* reason are what is used to rule over passion. This most likely calls back to Plato's comments on how passion needs to be controlled. Still, it sits well with Christian wisdom.

imagination this way because Scripture is filled with imagery in the form of metaphor. Linguists specializing in the study of languages tell us that metaphors happen when a person or group needs to describe something in a way no simple words can define.[8] For example, when trying to get information out of somebody who never gives anything up, we say it's like "squeezing blood from a stone." Linguists also tell us that imaginative language we create helps us try and express the inconceivable,[9] and, like with the metaphor I just gave, when enough of those expressions get into a culture, it creates something referred to as a "social imaginary," which acts like a basket or storehouse that we reach into all the time even without knowing it which then has the capacity to shape culture without us knowing it. So, when we read the metaphors in the Bible's poetic books (which make up a third of Scripture), we are reading how the authors have imagined God and his qualities to be through the inspiration of the Spirit. However, even in the narrative sections, imagery still captures our imagination, such as all the supernatural events in Exodus. We must make space in ourselves to conceptualize and ponder such imagery and what God is doing with it, especially since what is being said in the Bible comes from a distant time.

Perhaps the Christian imagination is like a garden where we make space for what God communicates to us as Scripture plants its images in us. When our thoughts are turned towards God, the Spirit tends them and causes them to bloom, sparking parts of us that need reawakening. The Christian imagination is a realization that, as Tolkien states, "there was an Eden on this very unhappy earth . . . we all long for it and are constantly glimpsing it: our whole nature at its best and least corrupted, its gentlest and most human."[10] We are still in exile, so to speak, but we "desire to return to our authentic home," the garden of our imagination turned

---

8. Reuland, "Working Memory," 101. Reuland notes that human language is unique and what separates us from every other species on the planet.

9. Reuland, "Working Memory," 101.

10. Loconte, *A Great War*, 131–132. Quoting from: *The Letters Of J. R. R. Tolkien*, 110–111, 151.

EMBRACING THE STRANGE

toward the words of the Bible can give us a fragment of our true home's light.[11]

In the above terms, it takes humility and courage to have an imagination. Using our Creator-endowed imagining helps us with the parts of God the Bible reveals that we can't quite comprehend, but it also makes room for the Word of God to reorient our thoughts. Having an imagination acknowledges that we can't yet know God exhaustively while helping lead us into the fear of the Lord (reverent wonder) because the imaginative process is often contemplative and anchored in humility. At the same time, it's also God's way of inviting us to "play."

IMAGINATION AND THE TRUTH

Now that we've discussed the concept of imagination, we should get back to Ezekiel's vision mentioned earlier in the chapter, which you may have been wondering about. How can a person apply their imagination to understanding such a passage of Scripture? We can get to that if we are willing to ask another question first: Is what Ezekiel saw in his vision real? Remember that one of the primary functions of the imagination is to help us express an idea that simple words can't convey properly or express the inconceivable. That doesn't mean that these imaginative "expressions" are fictional or merely symbols, even though we find a lot of symbolism in the Bible. They can also serve to de-symbolize, especially within Scripture, and be as good a guide to reality as rational arguments.[12]

We have to contend with something else, too, such as how truth relates to Scripture. One of the bedrock approaches in the West when it comes to holding up the Bible as authoritative is asserting and defending its truthfulness. This is because the Enlightenment period and Modernity—the offspring of the Enlightenment—notoriously

---

11. Loconte, *A Great War*, 131–132, The original quote speaks of why mythology and fiction were born. The human sub-creator, by creating these stories populated with magical and all sorts of imaginative creatures, is attempting to recall humanity's life before the fall.

12. Loconte, *A Hobbit, Wardrobe, And A Great War*, 128.

scrutinized the Bible's reliability based on their own philosophical standards. Much like how Jedi rose to meet the growing threat of the Sith, conservative, orthodox Christians combatted the standards of liberal theologians and historians with varying degrees of success based on similar objective and rationalistic tactics.[13] We say "varying degrees of success" because one of the unintended consequences of that dust-up was the rise of Christian fundamentalism, which, at present, only allows a strictly literal interpretation of the whole Bible, and sometimes the reading of only one translation of the Bible, the 1611 King James Version.

Yet, for whatever unintended harm may have been done, one of the best outcomes of defending the Bible's authority and truthfulness was that it exposed our cultural blinders. The Enlightenment and Modernity posited, in a way, that if information came from such a time in the past, such as before the scientific revolution, it must be untrue because that time was more primitive. Historians today say those in the Enlightenment believed they "possessed new knowledge and a new way of knowing which gave them a privileged position to judge the errors of the past."[14] For example, the 19th-century German liberal theologian Ernst Troeltsch praised the idea that no one thought as the ancients anymore and championed the popular sentiment that ancient beliefs regarding the accumulation of knowledge were problematic.[15] Therefore, Troeltsch advocated for only the humanity of Jesus and argued against traditional Christian doctrines such as the Trinity.[16] The problem with that, of course, was that he was using the ideas of his time, and much of that period was focused on the advancement of the human outside of revelation, faith, and tradition. If we remember what was said above, that the Christian imagination was our thoughts turned toward God, we can then see how easily it was for the people of Troeltsch's day to think as they did.

---

13. For a thorough look at this subject, see, Olson, *The Journey of Modern Theology*.
14. Olson, *The Journey of Modern Theology*, 17.
15. Olson, *The Journey of Modern Theology*, 186–87.
16. Olson, *The Journey of Modern Theology*, 187.

I bring all of this information up not to come across as a know-it-all but to say we haven't fully healed from the losses sustained in the eras of Enlightenment and Modernity. We still hear those same arguments in some circles, especially when it comes to particular views that are perceived to be human rights issues, like abortion. Even with the rise of Post-Modernist philosophy, which is another development of Western society, we are still coming to understand that we are wearing cultural blinders when it comes to reading the Bible. One could argue that the reverse is true: that the Bible was a product of a culture's perspective, and many have, but chances are that if you've accepted Christ, you at least trust what it testifies about Christ to be true. If that's the case, why not keep going? To be open to the biblical imagination, what the Bible says about reality in God's story, and to be available to its truthfulness is to recover our imagination, and I would argue the human imagination. We can say such things with confidence because if we accept that we are created in the image of God, our imaginations are meant to be turned toward him in the first place, and we can find this knowledge within Scripture.

WHAT'S OLD IS NEW

So, let's get back to how a person can apply their imagination to understanding such a passage of Scripture. In one straightforward way (and hopefully not reductively), Ezekiel's vision acts as a way to connect the imagination of the reader to the imagination of the writer and his original audience, the exiles. Remember that the imagination acts as a way to reason through specific things, and God speaks through his prophets to address particular circumstances. So, the reader must ask: what are the concerns of the exiles and the concerns of God that he is speaking to in this vision? Indeed, part of it had to do with being exiles. The Babylonians conquered Jerusalem, the capital of Judah, and then the conquerors deported many of the city's residents to places abroad. The exiles had no choice; it was leave or die.

So, while the part of the vision that makes up Ezekiel 1:15–22 is valuable, the use of the imagination can begin within the first three verses. To be an exile means to be displaced, again, usually against one's choice. Perhaps we can think about a time when we or someone we know had been displaced. What was the experience like for us or the person we know? What was it like to be ripped away from everything we or they knew? What was running through our head or our friend's head? Did we, or did they have any hope? In my experience, we mostly wait for our pastors to prompt these questions in a sermon, but asking questions like these in our personal readings is part of reasoning through something; it *is* using the imagination and is an excellent thing to do.

Another clue to the importance of this vision comes to us in the first section of verse three. It says, "The word of the LORD came to the priest Ezekiel, son of Buzi." Ezekiel's priestly identity adds a whole new depth of meaning to the significance of the vision. Jewish worship in Judah was centered around the Temple in Jerusalem. The Temple was where the Ark of the Covenant (which contained the stone tablets on which the Ten Commandments were written) was held. It was built by King Solomon as a house of the LORD. It was also the central site for many religious festivals and the most important day of the year, Yom Kippur, the Day of Atonement. However, in other Old Testament books describing the history of the exile, we find that the Temple was destroyed by the Babylonians (2 Kgs 25:9, which comes before Ezekiel in the OT). So, the way the Jews worshipped God and the ability of Ezekiel to carry out his duties was shattered. Although the first-time reader wouldn't know this, Ezekiel's priestly duty would have been at the altar and would have been ordained for that at the age of thirty, but he spent that birthday in exile.[17] At this point, we not only have a displaced people torn from the land they loved, but we also have a priest torn from the duties he had been preparing to do for so long. Therefore, we can't approach handling Ezekiel's vision in verses 15–22 with our imaginations unless we engage them with the surrounding context/reason of the vision first.

17. Sweeny, *Reading Ezekiel*, 26.

Embracing The Strange

Yet, we're still not done with the depth of the first three verses! Now that we have the information about what Ezekiel and the exiles are going through and can hopefully relate somewhat with them, we are treated to something else we can possibly relate to in the opening verses: God showing up. If you have been reading the Old Testament, starting from Genesis, you may be aware of how localized the faith of Israel was. We know that God had promised Abraham that his descendants would be a blessing to the nations (Gen 12:3). But for the most part, the religion and activity of God with Israel had been regionally specific (not counting the Exodus).[18] Israel, after all, is the promised land. Now that this land had been taken away from them, it was unclear how it would impact the relationship between the exiled people of Israel with God and their worship of him. Through the heavens opening up to Ezekiel on the banks of a foreign river, the exiles would soon learn, and the reader finds out that God is not constrained to physical borders.

One could argue, however, that they had the Torah. The exiles knew that Yahweh was not bound by land since he created the world and because God had promised the Israelites that he would always be their God. They would always be his people (Exod 6:7). But it is one thing to read of God's promises and another to experience him fulfilling them, and that's part of what's happening for Ezekiel.

This is not to say nothing about the fact that exile was the punishment for breaking the covenant with God. Through the prophets, Yahweh gave enough warning to the people of Israel and Judah about what would happen if they continued to stray from the covenant. But where people fail to honor God, he faithfully honors himself and his creatures. Neither land nor sin can withstand the activity and love of God; they only inhibit us. Armed with this information, we can think about how the situation of the exiles has mirrored our own lives. How have rebellion and disobedience inhibited our lives, and yet we still find that God shows up? This is the contemplative component of the imagination. We reflect, and in that reflection, we take what happened and (with the

---

18. Martens, *God's Design*, 114–15. Martens discusses the importance of the land with respect to several promises God makes to Israel's patriarchs.

The Garden of Scripture

process of imagination) try to put it into words only to fall back on the biblical words that contain immense meaning, such as grace and salvation. The reader, then, is not just to read the three verses with a far-off historical lens but with the awareness that the people who went through things in Scripture were flesh and blood people, just like we are flesh and blood people.

Ezekiel's vision is not done stirring the reader's imagination; something in the next verse is integral to the scriptural imaginary across both Testaments. Verse four says, "As I looked, a stormy wind came out of the north: a great cloud with brightness around it and fire flashing forth continually, and in the middle of the fire, something like gleaming amber." The storm imagery represents what is called a theophany, an event where the presence of God is made visibly (and audibly) manifest, and they are often physical encounters. A similar occurrence happens in Exodus 19 when the presence of God descends upon Mount Sinai to the terrified witness of the Israelite encampment. Similarly, in Job 38, God dramatically visits Job as a whirlwind and overwhelms the man and his so-called "friends" with divine wisdom. The Psalms also frequently speak of God's stormy appearances and qualities (Ps 18, 77). However, the next most similar event happens in Acts 2 when the Holy Spirit arrives as a "violent wind" in the upper room, and tongues of fire appear over the heads of everyone there (Acts 2:1–4). The description of God in this form is part of the biblical imaginary, images that inhabit Scripture continually. Tim Mackie, co-founder of the ministry BibleProject, likes to refer to the things found in the biblical imaginary as "hyperlinks" because Scripture's original readers would have known the significance of how some of the things they witnessed or read would have called back to other experiences in Scripture. That's why those who first read the book of Acts would have understood the significance of God's Spirit visiting in such an appearance and could link it back to several Old Testament passages.

The stormy passages above are something that I've tried to envision several times, particularly the passage in Exodus 19, and maybe it's because of having enjoyed storms as a child. Still, I've

EMBRACING THE STRANGE

never seen a storm that involves fire as well. In Deuteronomy 5, when Moses recounted that event, he said the Israelites were so overwhelmed by seeing God that way they felt they'd die hearing his voice (Deut 5:25). If we think about what a severe storm is like, we can recall how multi-sensory they are. Not only would there have been the visual and auditory elements, but there would have also been the tactile element of feeling the wind against their skin and whatever else the wind was kicking up. Since the Bible says fire was involved, people could feel the heat. What kind of response do you think such an experience would trigger within you? I sometimes wonder if I'd act the same way or be like Moses and go up to the mountain and speak with God. Verse four, then, does something to complement the first three verses. If the first three verses show that God is not bound by land and disobedience and will still show up to exiles in their displacement, then the storm imagery illustrates that he is doing his activity in power and authority.[19] Yahweh is not just the God of Israel anymore for them; they were learning in real-time that he is the God of the cosmos.

The learning in real time that God is God for the people of the Old Testament is something that we may not have ever considered before or at least upon the first reading. God is inviting us into the story through the words on the pages of our Bibles, much like any author would. But because Christians worship the same God as the exiles, we can learn the same things about God as they learned when it was actually happening to them. Regarding the storm imagery that Ezekiel is speaking about, remember that it is part of theophany, an encounter. The translation may say "vision," but the Hebrew implies an encounter, meaning the imagery relays something happening just as they are intended to do in many circumstances.[20] And I must give us a gentle reminder again that imagery and metaphor are the imagination helping us process inconceivable things. In that case, it could be that Ezekiel was seeing

---

19. Odell, *Ezekiel*, 18. Odell states that the question for the exiles wouldn't be about a local gods mobility around surrounding regions, but if that local god had any power and authority in another land.

20. Odell, *Ezekiel*, 13.

something even more spectacular than what could be contained by his description. It would take a humble and courageous imagination to accept that, but that is what God is asking us to do.

Indeed, God is asking us to use the capacity of our imaginations throughout the rest of the chapter as well. Out of the storm comes the throne-chariot of God, supported by beings with the face of a human, lion, eagle, and ox that have powerful significance not only in the biblical imagination but also in the imagination of the Ancient Near East as respective lords of creation. Those beings are situated under God to show his authority over them no matter where he is. Their wings touch, recalling the Ark of the Covenant imagery, where the cherubim's wings touch and form the "mercy seat." These four creatures also appear in the book of Revelation, where they serve and worship before God. In this passage, though, they shine like burnished bronze, another allusion to the Ark's design. Had they been in the Temple, they'd be reflecting the light of the seven lamps in the holy of holies, filling the room in light. The chariot's wheels and their material also tell our imaginations that their construction is to reflect and even refract light like a jewel, casting prismatic light everywhere.

Ezekiel is witnessing the glory of God, his divine essence soaking creation in light as his power moves throughout creation and as he exercises judgment upon the earth.[21] The throne-chariot and the figure representing God atop it is *enormous*, and as Ezekiel says, it is "*awesome*" (1:18) in the most technical sense of the word, bringing on the fear of the Lord, which means to be in reverent awe of him.

Therefore, when we read passages like Ezekiel 1, which communicates the glory of God upon the earth, and when it shares that those who witnessed such things, it should prompt us to think a little deeper, to maybe try and visualize in our mind the imagery that is being described and reflect on what it brings to mind about God. This doesn't mean we let our thoughts get carried away from the core message; we do need to discipline our imagination, but we should be reading with our whole person and directed toward God.

21. Odell, *Ezekiel*, 18.

And who knows, maybe when we read like this, we will find that our imaginations will grow and spill out into other areas. Perhaps we will see that we can't help but create stories that similarly reflect the glory of God in a way that doesn't have to be spelled out in front of us. Creating worlds deeply impacted by faith in God can bring as it did with Lewis, Tolkien, and L'Engle. Maybe reading like this has already caused janitors to become poets and those who mumble to become singers of great songs. And, perhaps, it has helped those who thought they were alone in their thoughts about God find they are actually much-needed sages.

4

Illusions and Fullness

An enchanted Christian social imaginary will involve revisiting what it means to be human and the nature of the divine–human relationship.

—Cheryl Bridges Johns[1]

I AM A FAN of the ocean, particularly the northeast Atlantic, where I spent many summers and lived for six years. Whenever possible, I would spend a whole day at the beach swimming, even though the water temperature averaged sixty degrees. When I got into my late teens and early twenties, I preferred to walk along the beach in the evening and look out at the ocean as if it had an answer I was looking for. I have to admit that I was looking for something. I was looking for purpose and inspiration to figure out who I was and thinking that, at any point, all the answers would pop into my head if I stared out at the horizon long enough. It didn't happen, and it didn't happen because I wasn't looking in the right place.

So, where did I find those answers? It sounds cliché, but I found purpose and inspiration in reading Scripture and discovered who I was when I gave myself to Christ. And something happens; it's like a path, a process, or a paradox. The more I give up my

---

1. Johns, *Re-Enchanting the Text*, 43.

ILLUSIONS AND FULLNESS

life to Christ, the more I discover who I am. It's a continual growth in understanding my identity in Jesus.

Nevertheless, there are some things my time at the beach taught me. I found that crabs prefer to hide under seaweed on the clustered rocks by the water. I discovered that if shattered glass is in the sea long enough, it becomes smooth around the edges and strangely captivating to the eye, so much so that people collect the glass. I also learned that water often magnifies what's beneath it, giving the illusion that what's on the bottom is only a few inches or less from the water's surface. As a child, I would test that illusion frequently in tidepools, thinking them to be only a few inches deep, but I often found that the water would go up to my knee. In school, we learn things under the water; even the surface under the water looks larger and closer because the light is being refracted, not traveling in a straight line anymore, slowing down, which causes magnification. Thus, the illusion comes to life.

In my time as a student, minister, and teacher, I've observed that a lot of people, both Christians and non-Christians, sometimes view the Bible the same way as the tidepool. Those who pick up the Bible for the first time, or even veterans, might see something beautiful, like one would with the mini eco-systems in a tidepool, and reach their hand in only to find they are in over their head, barely treading water. However, people who oppose Christianity and have already made up their minds about it and what they've heard the Bible says only see the illusion of shallowness and don't even bother to reach in.

PROBLEMS WITH ILLUSIONS

I think the illusion partly happens because we don't always know how much of the Bible we should take literally. But the word "literally" is casually thrown around so often that we must try to discern what the word means in the sense of interpreting the Bible. That is no easy task because it has been bogged down by so much historical baggage from the last hundred and fifty years. Typically, a literal reading of Scripture is supposed to be tied to a type of interpretation

THE GARDEN OF SCRIPTURE

called the historical-grammatical method that seeks to discern the meaning of a passage as the author intended it to be understood. Using this method, the setting and circumstances of why the biblical book was written need to be identified, including the historical aspect. The other element, the grammatical, determines what the words and sentences in a passage mean and what genre it is written in so that the passage can be "plainly" communicated.

Somewhere along the way, however, wires must have gotten crossed because taking the text "literally" has become weaponized. It is sad to say that the weaponization of the word has occurred within Christianity, with its own members warring against each other. Much ink has been spilled on trying to explain why it happened. Some say it's because the "literal" historical-grammatical interpretation protects the truth God reveals in Scripture. However, critics say that Christians who interpret using the method refuse to reflect upon what science reveals about the natural world. Like many conflicts, stereotyping came into play, making matters worse.

"You actually believe God made the world in six literal days? You, poor dear. I hope you come out of your cave soon."

"You don't believe the number the Bible gives for the Israelites in the wilderness is accurate? I hear hell is hot this time of year."

The problem is it seems like some Christians gave into the stereotypes. Eventually, those Christians began to interpret the Bible and apply things to their faith that a "literal" interpretation was never meant for us to apply. Suddenly, the Hebrew cosmology of a three-tiered creation seen in Hannah's prayer, depicting a flat world, must be applied to our time despite a wealth of information that proves otherwise. However, others began dismissing parts of the Bible that a "literal" interpretation was meant for us to apply, such as belief in the resurrection of Jesus and sexual integrity.[2] And now, a literal interpretation is synonymous with not allowing any other interpretive methods because they're seen as sinful or worldly by those whose idea of literal interpretation is infused

2. The disbelief in the resurrection has existed since at least Enlightenment in some capacity but has become more widespread among those who promote Jesus only for his moral and ethical teachings.

with rigid dogmatism. And those who have a much more nuanced view of a literal view are looked down upon. Then politics had to be injected, and that never helped anything. What's worse is that the loudest voices in the room are the ones that are on the extreme fringes of each side, each vying for control of the "true" message of the Bible. Interestingly, one part of Christianity always tries to speak for the whole of Christianity.[3]

I bring all of this up because it has made Bible reading more difficult for many people who already struggle, it makes it harder for those who are called to teach, and it turns people off from even picking up the Bible; it shouldn't be like this. In the secular world, humanity has found many ways to maim and kill one another, but in Christianity, depending on who we listen to, it can seem like we are acquiring a lot of methods to maim and kill our faith.

The fight over a literal interpretation is not the only thing that can make a person feel like they're in over their head. There is also the problem of time. The excuse of not having enough time often reflects the deeper issue of a lack of desire to study Scripture; some would instead do other things that give a more instantaneous reward. However, adults also have a lot of essential responsibilities such as work, managing finances, raising children, etc. Realistically, all of that is often time-consuming, if not exhausting, and trying to add a sincere reading of the Bible on top of everything is daunting. A mature believer may say that if a person starts their day with reading, it will put them in the right frame to tackle the rest of the day's tasks. That is true, but they probably didn't start out that way.

Our obsession with time, not having enough, and not having good quality is, of course, symptomatic of our era. So many books and people tell us to slow down, reprioritize, simplify, and

---

3. Lewis, *God In The Dock*, 217. In an essay featured in the book, Lewis confronts the idea of a Christian political party in England noting it wouldn't be successful because as soon as it makes certain accommodations or takes money from non-Christian financiers, it would cease being Christian. It also wouldn't be able to speak for the whole of Christianity simply because English Christianity is only part of the body of Christ, not the whole thing. The same can be said for Christian denominations who try to control the definition of a "true" interpretation of the Bible.

be mindful. Yet, we might not have enough time to read or listen to those voices. However, let's say we do listen, and we then decide to read for fifteen minutes, but then we are overcome with the thought of that not being *enough* time. We wonder, *is that even enough time to gain a worthwhile understanding of God? Can I get to know God more in just fifteen minutes?* My answer is yes. God can do more in fifteen minutes than we can imagine, even if we don't realize it until later. But we have to be okay with that small amount of time.

The reason I believe we need to be okay with only being able to give God a small amount of our time has to do with motive. When we reach our hand into the tidepool, our motive is to grab what's at the bottom because we are eager to get an up-close look at whatever the object is, be it a starfish or a periwinkle shell; we're curious. We will only learn so much through mere curiosity; we learn much more through faithful, consistent, and committed curiosity. The award for that accrues over time, and suddenly, we find we know that object at the bottom of the tidepool intimately. The dedication to reading the Bible consistently, even if it's only for a short amount of time, is like that, but only sort of. It is only "sort of" like that because even though God is the object of our faith and study, and we are getting to know him more intimately, God is not an object like a periwinkle shell or a sand dollar. Instead, he reveals that we are one of his most prized objects and demonstrates how intimately he already knows us. So, over time, our motive must shift from genuine curiosity to one that accepts and tries to understand how God uses the Bible to form his people into an object, a living vessel that reflects his glory.

The issue of time can be healed when the above motive shifts along with the petition to God for more time. God is perfectly able to move us out of what restricts us from him, whatever our excuses, especially in the hyper-distracted West. Our job is to relent, sacrifice, and use that time wisely. Part of using time wisely is coming to terms with the fact that we will not instantaneously learn everything we need to know about the Bible and what God is saying to us in one reading. When we heed that wisdom, we

ILLUSIONS AND FULLNESS

become like the trusty characters in Jesus' parable of the talents. In the parable, Jesus tells his disciples that a person who owns a lot of property needs to head out of town, so he asks three of his workers to manage the property, giving one worker five talents (an amount of money equal to 75 years' wages), the second worker two talents, and the third worker one talent. While the property manager was away, the two with the most money invested what they had in unnamed things and doubled the amount given to them. When the property owner returns and the first two workers tell him the good news, he rewards them with more responsibility, which is joyfully received. However, the worker with only one talent buried the money in the field and attacked the property owner's character upon his return (Matt 28:14–28). The parable ends with that worker being fired and evicted from the property. Jesus' lesson is that those who receive from God and put it into action will receive more from him. When we ask God for more time to get closer to him, he'll give it to us.

JOHN AND RACHEL

Indeed, it will take time to read the Bible, as it should. Relationships take time, and finite humans encounter the infinite God in Scripture. We will not master the Bible over our lifetime either, even if we better understand it toward the end of our lives. That means it will not always be simple. We should probably be wary when people say the Bible has a "simple teaching" about God. A "simple teaching" is like looking at a flower and saying, "This is a flower." Though it is true that the Gospel, the message of Christ, is simple enough for a child to understand, it by no means stays simple but grows more profound the more we mature as readers. So, while some are intent on staying at a simple teaching, the Bible continues to the depths God meant it for. It can be kind of like John and Rachel's story here:

John was strolling through his neighborhood on a splendid midsummer evening. As he climbed a small hill, he saw a bush dotted with vibrant red shapes. The closer John came to it, the more he realized it was a rose bush. John then noticed that the owner of the home where the rose bush was, an older woman who appeared to be in her mid-fifties, was watering the lawn. John picked up his stride to reach her before she finished and went inside.

"Excuse me," John said, panting.

"Hello," she returned warmly. "You're John, right?"

"Yes, that's right," he returned as he caught his breath. "I apologize; I don't believe I've ever asked you your name."

The woman chucked and batted a hand at him. "Don't worry, I'm afraid I'm somewhat of a busybody, but my name is Beverly. Oh, but I prefer Bev."

"Excellent," John replied. "It's a pleasure to meet you. Listen, I stopped by because I was wondering if I could get a closer look at the rose bush? It's magnificent!"

"Of course," she said, smiling warmly again at him while waving him over.

The roses were even better up close. Examining the lushness and vitality of the rose petals, John was mesmerized. "I don't believe I've ever seen such a healthy rose bush before," he exclaimed.

"Ah, yes," Bev replied kindly. "I bought them at a nursery on the other side of town at the recommendation of a friend. It's called Vera's."

Still entranced by the roses, John replied, "I wouldn't mind having these in my yard as well."

"I can give you the address if you'd like? The owner is wonderful! She's younger than I thought she'd be but packed full of knowledge," said Bev.

Bev's question put John on the spot, and he had to think it over briefly. John wondered if he said he wanted a rose bush like the one in front of him because he really desired it or said it because he was being friendly. He at least decided to take the address.

"Yes, thank you," he replied as he got out his phone to type in the address.

When she finished, John politely said goodbye and continued his evening walk.

Illusions and Fullness

Later in the evening, as John was shaving after a shower, he found his mind becoming fixated on the rose bush again. He'd been telling the truth when he said they were magnificent. Perhaps it would be nice to step out into his yard and see something like that daily; maintaining them would be worth the effort. John then determined that he'd visit the nursery the next day, talk to the owner, and decide.

The following morning, John ate his breakfast, got dressed, and made good on the decision the night before to visit Vera's. He pulled up the address on his phone's navigation app and found it was only fifteen minutes from his home. Finally arriving, John discovered a modest-sized shop with an attached greenhouse a shade larger. He entered, and what he found surprised him. So many healthy flowers, both common and uncommon, were all arranged in humble but enchanting displays. Colors popped out at him from every direction, and plants in the greenhouse resembled a picturesque tropical island; there was even a place in the back of the property filled with young trees and various shrubs. It reminded John of the imagery in C. S. Lewis's *Perelandra,* which he read back in college. No wonder the rose bush appeared so wonderful, coming from a place like this!

John then tried to track down the owner. The nursery was a bit busy with it being a weekend, but it wasn't crowded. He asked one employee at the cash register, a young college-aged boy if he knew where the owner was. The boy was unsure and told him to ask the assistant manager who was in the greenhouse. Stepping down in the greenhouse, he spotted a young woman in a forest green polo with a badge bearing the name "Kristen."

"Excuse me," he said, walking up to her. "The cashier told me you might know where I could find the owner."

The young Kristen looked up at him politely but uneasily. "Yes, she's out in the back," she replied. "I can take you to her."

"Thank you," John replied as friendly as he could.

As the two walked back into the shop, where the doors leading to the back part of the property were, John tried to strike up some small talk.

"So, how long have you been working here?" John asked.

"Oh, about two years," she replied casually.

"Do you like it?"

"Yeah, I do. My aunt is the owner. Yay, nepotism!" She said jokingly.

They passed through the double doors into a sizable open-air but fenced-in area. Kristen spied around quickly and spotted her aunt, who had her back to them and was inspecting a few pots containing stargazer lilies. She then continued to escort John toward the woman.

"Aunt Rachel?" Kristen called out.

The woman turned around, revealing her somewhat bookish appearance, but had sun-kissed skin, deep brown hair, and a welcoming smile. To John's embarrassment, he found himself quite taken with her looks.

"Aunt Rachel," Kristen said again as they approached her. "I think this man had a few questions for you."

"How can I help you," she asked with a soft yet assertive voice, removing her glasses.

She had large and captivating blue eyes. John tried not to stare. "Hi, thank you. This place was recommended by my neighbor, Bev."

"Oh, I love Bev!" Rachel replied. "She is a dream customer and so pleasant."

"Well," John continued, "I saw the rose bush in her yard, and I couldn't stop thinking about it. To be honest, I don't think about flowers that much. I'm not exactly one for gardening, but the rose bush was brilliant, and she told me she got the bulbs from here. So, I thought I'd come by and check this place out and ask why those roses looked so good."

Rachel blushed somewhat at his comments. "Well, a lot of that has to do with the gardener, but our website offers a lot of information on how to tend a garden."

"I see. Did you go to school for all of this?" He asked awkwardly.

"Not exactly," Rachel replied. "I spent my summers with my grandmother, *the* "Vera" in Vera's Nursey, and she's the one who taught me all I know. Although, to be fair, she was a botanist turned horticulturalist."

"Does she work here as well," John asked.

Rachel's face became a bit downcast at the question, which made John feel a little stupid.

"No," she said. "Unfortunately, she passed away a few years after I got out of college," she trailed off. "But this shop is dedicated to her legacy."

After a few more minutes of conversation, John decided to buy a bulb of a rose bush and try his hand at growing it. When he arrived home, he looked up the store's website and followed its instructions on properly planting and maintaining it to ensure growth. Over the next two weeks, he watched it as it grew, noticing several healthy buds. John also thought of Rachel and how there was more of a story behind her relationship with her grandmother based on her solemn response to his question.

A few more days went by, and over that time, he prepared a place in his backyard to plant more flowers, following the website's instructions. While genuinely wanting to grow more things, he also wanted to see Rachel again. When the garden bed was finished, he returned to Vera's Nursery. John was able to track her down and thanked her for the success he experienced. He then asked if she had any advice on what else he could plant as a beginner, to which she suggested Daylilies. John did something else, though, something as risky as planting roses with no experience; he asked her out for coffee. Although she eyed him carefully when he asked, Rachel agreed.

To John's amazement, they met several more times after their coffee date. During one meeting in particular, Rachel decided to share more about the relationship between her and her Grandmother, Vera. The relationship the two shared wasn't just based on gardening but on the bond of love. Rachel's grandmother passed on her wisdom as well as her skills. When she wasn't with her grandmother in the summer, they'd talk on the phone several times a week. Rachel even shared how she'd gotten pregnant in college, thinking her grandmother was going to kill her, and admitted her parents were furious. Vera was upset with her, naturally, but continued to offer the love she always had. Then, through tears, Rachel recounted the care her grandmother gave her when she went through the devastation of miscarrying the pregnancy.

That admittance by Rachel marked a turning point in John's relationship with her; it was a brave step to take in sharing with him. John knew then that he wanted to marry Rachel, and after a few more months, he popped the question, to which she answered with an excited "Yes!"

Soon after their marriage, the imagery of *Perelandra* became a reality. Rachel transformed his yard into a paradise. No, it was *their* yard now, *their* paradise.

In this story, John avoided the error of thinking he had all of the information he needed about the roses just by looking at them. Had he not taken the time to go on the journey of finding the owner of the nursery, he would have missed out on a world of meaning, on a grand story that spans generations, and John would have missed out on the person he'd spend the rest of his life with. John was faithful to his journey even though it led him away from himself and to another. However, he also finds a more complete version of himself when he develops a relationship with Rachel. Although it is not a perfect example, the story illustrates that a faithful reading—which keeps context in mind—of the Bible leads us away from ourselves and to the God who revealed himself in it. Yet, the more we are led away from ourselves and to God, the more we find a complete version of ourselves as we find that God has authored us. Like John and Rachel's story and the way flowers unfold as they bloom, the story of Scripture unfolds as we take the steps that lead beyond the surface of a "simple teaching." We must be humble then and not rush to conclusions, nor should we be intent on thinking we will understand everything correctly when the Bible is meant to consume a lifetime of study.

ILLUSIONS AND FULLNESS

PRISMATIC FULLNESS

The unfolding of meaning in the Bible reflects another thing about God. In chapter 3 of Ephesians, the Apostle Paul says, "Through the church the wisdom of God in its rich variety might now be made known to the rulers and authorities in the heavenly places" (Eph 3:10). The word Paul uses for "rich variety," which can also be translated as "manifold," is the Greek word *polypoikilos*. The word can mean many-sided or many-colored. We can think of God's wisdom then as a jewel with many facets. When light passes through this jewel, the eye is treated to seeing the color spectrum when it's cast onto a surface. The difference, though, is that God emits his own light. So, in this sense, he is both the jewel and the light. What God gives us in Scripture is layered; it is multifaceted because he is multifaceted, but everything he gives us leads to himself. That is why we must be careful of people who teach their method of reading Scripture as the only valid method and disregard what others can contribute. Not only does it smack of fundamentalism, which is more of an attitude than a denomination, but it isn't humble either. God is more significant than even the most faithful reading we can devise.

That doesn't mean that we shouldn't strive for faithful reading or aim for the truth. The prismatic brilliance of Scripture is not something that sets out to defeat our efforts. Sometimes, we may feel in over our heads, realizing the tidepool we reached into has become the ocean, but what may help us is that God is the ocean. Instead of thinking we are surrounded by the sea and about to drown, we can find that we are swimming in the fullness of God. The jewel doesn't just reveal light as layers of colors; it demonstrates light is *full* of color. So, perhaps we need a good understanding of God's fullness as readers of the Bible.

Understanding God's fullness might look like what theologian and pastor Tony Richie discusses in his book *Essentials of Pentecostal Theology*. In it, he attempts to trace out the "theology of fullness" to support the Pentecostal practice of Spirit-baptism. While defending such a doctrine is not the focus of this section (even though I'm a Pentecostal Christian), Richie guides readers of the Bible by pointing out how the language of "filling" is a prominent and favored figure of speech throughout Scripture, especially relating to divine truth and spiritual experience.[4] To do this, he teases it out in a few ways. First, Richie points out how God fills creation, citing several verses such as Numbers 14:21, where God says, "Nevertheless—as I live, and as all the earth shall be filled with the glory of the LORD."[5] The author then points out that God even fills the homes of his people and their mouths with praise (Neh 9:25, Ps 71:8).

The nature of filling continues all the way through the New Testament in the disciples and onlookers reactions to Christ's miracles and provision (Luke 5:26, John 2:7). Then, filling takes on another dimension in the book of Acts as the disciples are filled with the Holy Spirit who empowers them to preach the Gospel boldly and perform signs and wonders (Acts 2:1-4, 3:1-8, 5:12-16, 8:4-13, 9:40-41, etc.). Many whom the Apostles encountered, however, also experienced a filling/baptism of the Spirit, such as when Peter and John ministered to the same Samaritans as Philip (8:14-17) and when Cornelius came into the faith through Peter's preaching (10:44-46).[6] Richie gives several other examples, but his work recalls the words of King David when he says, "Where can I go from your spirit? Or where can I flee from your presence? If I ascend to heaven, you are there; if I make my bed in Sheol, you are there" (Ps 139:7-8).

On the other hand, we must also acknowledge that we can be filled in different ways that don't reflect God. To see this, we only need to look back to Genesis 1. At the end of the chapter, God gives Adam and Eve the divine mandate to "be fruitful and multiply and fill the earth and subdue it" (Gen 1:28). Instead, they fill the earth with violence because they disobeyed God's command of not eating from the tree of the knowledge of good and evil.[7]

---

4. Richie, *Essentials of Pentecostal Theology*, 133.
5. Richie, *Essentials of Pentecostal Theology*, 133.
6. Richie, *Essentials of Pentecostal Theology*, 133.
7. Richie, *Essentials of Pentecostal Theology*, 133.

Illusions and Fullness

This indicates that it turns into negative behavior when humanity tries to supplement God's fullness for their own. For example, when coming across Jesus, religious leaders were "filled with wrath (Luke 4:28)." The infilling of rage would continue as they schemed and devised (the harmful use of imagination) how to arrest and execute Jesus, which eventually culminated with his execution.

As the gospels tell us, however, Jesus is resurrected, thereby defeating sin, the power of death, and Satan. He then bestows his promise of the Spirit's coming (Acts 1:8), *fulfilled* in Acts 2. While we see miraculous signs performed by the Apostles through the power of the Spirit throughout the book of Acts, the Holy Spirit is given to all believers. He inhabits our lives and pours out God's love into our hearts (Eph 1:13, Rom 5:5); He is "God with us." The primary activity of the Holy Spirit in our lives is to sanctify and form our characters to resemble Christ, along with empowering our witness of Jesus. We are pressed by the Apostles to keep in step with the Spirit's guidance (Gal 5:25), and in this way, we can be victorious over the works of the flesh that seek to fill us with the desires of a fallen world.

Nevertheless, we still see through a mirror darkly, as Paul says (1 Cor 13:12). We only know in part, so we don't always understand we are surrounded by the fullness of God. This is because even though Jesus inaugurated the Kingdom of God at his resurrection, his return will fully realize the Kingdom of God. As the Apostle John wrote, "Beloved, we are God's children now; what we will be has not yet been revealed. What we do know is this: when he is revealed, we will be like him, for we will see him as he is" (1 John 3:3). That is why, as readers of the Bible, we need to be dependent on the leading and filling of the Spirit of God. It's in this filling and dependence that we experience the fullness of God in this life and in Scripture, in its rich variety, so that we can prepare for the face-to-face fullness of God in the eternal life to come.

As we grasp this fullness of God, which is experienced both temporally and spiritually over our whole life, the illusion begins to fade, and the truth becomes clear because we are consistently learning. The sea we had mistaken for a tidepool and had become

THE GARDEN OF SCRIPTURE

over our heads then suddenly turns into the water of life whose depths we humbly explore.

5

A Disruptive God

For as the surest source of destruction to men is to obey themselves, so the only haven of safety is to have no other will, no other wisdom, than to follow the Lord wherever he leads.[1]

—JOHN CALVIN

MY FAVORITE TIME OF the year, at this stage of life, is Spring. The budding of trees, the blossoming of flowers, and the scent of warming earth arrive in perfect accordance with Easter as if to add an exclamation point to celebrating the resurrection of Christ. The only thing that disrupts this joy is bees. Although I'm aware that bees are vital to Spring, nothing hampers my enjoyment of the outdoors more than a bee intruding into my airspace. I wouldn't say I'm deathly afraid of them, but let's just say I turn into a master of an unknown martial art when one buzzes too close. My aversion to them probably stems from two traumatic experiences of being stung as a child. Both times I had been stung, I never even noticed the bees had landed on me, stealthy little jerks. But bees are pollinators who help bring out the beauty of creation, so I must tolerate their disruption of my life.

1. Calvin, *Christian Religion*, 7.

The Bible likewise disrupts our lives. Truthfully, Scripture should disrupt our sensibilities as they tend to put us in a stupor. In his book *Sanctifying Interpretation*, Chris Green argues that "we have to learn to read and reread in ways that trouble and thwart us."[2] When we do this, Green says we force ourselves into participation with Christ and thereby into the wisdom God uses to shape us, which is his own wisdom.[3] We can ask, then, what is terrifying? How does God use his wisdom to shape us in a way that forces us into participation with Jesus? I believe the answer comes through one word, redemption.

PREFERRED REDEMPTION

The story of the Bible is often described as God performing salvific acts to redeem humanity, which culminates at the cross. Yet, we need to be careful of how we think about redemption. In popular media, redemption is portrayed as the idea of someone who's received justice after a wrong has been committed against them or they have been falsely accused of a crime. They've had to patiently endure while they've worked to restore and vindicate their reputation.

The film *The Shawshank Redemption*, based on a short story written by Stephen King, is the perfect example of the popular conception of redemption. In the story, the main character, Andy Dufresne, is accused of murdering his wife and her apparent lover. A jury finds Dufresne guilty, and he is sentenced to life in prison, serving his time at Shawshank Penitentiary. A little into his sentence, however, the guards and eventually the warden learn of Andy's financial skills because of his former career as a banker. Andy agrees to help guards through their difficulties and reluctantly assists the warden in "cooking the books" of the prison's accounts. As it turns out, the warden had been lending the prisoners to developers as a source of cheap labor and had to find a way to

---

2. Green, *Sanctifying Interpretation*, 162.
3. Green, *Sanctifying Interpretation*, 162.

A DISRUPTIVE GOD

account for the money. After some time, Andy meets a new prisoner, Tommy, whom he helps earn a G.E.D. The young man confesses to Dufresne that he might know who actually committed the crime Andy was convicted of. Believing Tommy, Andy approaches the warden about Tommy's evidence. However, after feigning to look into matters, the warden assassinates Tommy to keep Andy around so he can continue to handle the prison's accounts.

The warden's assassination order becomes the lynchpin in Andy's determination to escape. He had been digging a tunnel with a rock hammer for over two decades and finally asked his trusting friend, Red, to supply him with a rope. During an intense thunderstorm, Andy climbs through the tunnel he made and enters the prison's sewer, where, according to Red, "Andy crawled to freedom through five-hundred yards of sh— smelling foulness I can't even imagine."[4] The next shot is a climactic scene of victory where Andy Dufresne cleanses himself in the pouring rain, tasting the sweetness of freedom. However, Andy didn't escape empty-handed. He used the rope he asked for to drag the prison ledgers behind him, which had been sealed in plastic. The next day, after his escape, he uses the false alias on the prison account to withdraw hundreds of thousands of dollars and then mails the ledger to the newspaper. The following few scenes show the police arriving at the prison to arrest the warden and the guards. Redeemed, Andy then travels to Mexico to live out his dream.

As great as *The Shawshank Redemption* is, its message of redemption is not the same as that within the Bible. In the film, Andy is wrongly convicted because the justice system fails and keeps failing him; no one is seeking justice on his behalf, so Andy has to take matters into his own hands; he redeems himself. While it is a powerful example of perseverance, the film's portrayal of redemption is over-romanticized, like the ideal of the self-made man. Andy's redemption is well deserved, and the film's popularity makes us comfortable with the idea that his story is how redemption should be viewed.

4. Darabont, *The Shawshank Redemption*.

The story of Scripture, however, displays redemption with a vast difference. It does it in a manner that makes onlookers say, "Um, excuse me. What?" That is to say, biblical redemption is uncomfortable to almost everyone, especially to the people who saw Jesus interacting with outcasts. "If this man were a prophet," Simon the Pharisee says, "he would have known who and what kind of woman this is who is touching him—that she is a sinner" (Luke 7:39). Another Pharisee asks, "Why does your teacher [Jesus] eat with tax collectors and sinners" (Matt 9:11)? With the gospel's negative depiction of them, it's easy to say that Pharisees would think and say things like that, but what about the things we say behind closed doors or think to ourselves about who deserves what? We may be wise to consider what J. R. R. Tolkien communicated through the character of Gandalf, who tells Frodo, "Many that live deserve death. And some that die deserve life. Can you give it to them? Then do not be too eager to deal out death in judgment."[5]

Gandalf's question harkens to how Christians should examine redemption in light of Scripture. Indeed, the Bible subverts our notions of who redemption is given. It can be seen in the story of the 1820s lawyer Jackson Alexander:

Distant thunder rolled as Jackson and his two army escorts leisurely rode their horses to a Cherokee settlement in north Georgia on a forested trail. Rainwater dripped off his wide-brimmed hat, and he quietly sang to himself,

> "All I ask in this creation
> Is a pretty little wife and a big plantation
> Way up yonder in the Cherokee Nation."

Before they arrived there, however, they'd need to meet up with a local regiment of soldiers stationed on the way so that it would be enough to intimidate the Cherokee, hopefully sending the signal that their time on the land was up. It was the white man's turn, and Jackson felt it was his and his other white Americans' burden to make this land the greatest among the nations. He, in

---

5. Tolkien, *The Lord of the Rings*, 58.

A Disruptive God

fact, believed it was a mandate from God. For that reason, Jackson took pride in what he did.

Jackson had learned at the battle of Tippecanoe just several years earlier, where he achieved the rank of Sargent, that the natives of this land would never develop it to its God-given potential and would remain godless pagans like Tecumseh's ill-fated brother who claimed to be a prophet. Even though he'd fought heroically and achieved admirable esteem in the military, Jackson's heart was always with the law. When things died down in the western parts of the US territory, Jackson returned to practicing the law and specialized in finding loopholes in the treaties the country had made with the natives, and he was good at it. Jackson was relentless in this work, accompanied by an uncanny zeal in his beliefs, and he got the results his superiors wanted, which launched him into a highly reputable status among his peers.

That wasn't enough for him, though. Jackson also believed it was his responsibility to show up in person to pressure and instigate whatever action was needed to remove the tribes from where they lived. If that meant he had to clap a few people in irons, liberate children from their parents, or even provoke an armed skirmish, so be it. Jackson even approved of the recent hanging of a captured Cherokee man. The man was arrested on trumped-up charges, but he represented a danger against the proper order of things, especially after that man gave such an impassioned speech in his own defense. He'd never forget the sound of that Indian's neck snapping when he dropped from the gallows. To Jackson, it sounded like the future.

The forest cleared about a hundred feet in front of the three, and Alexander saw that the sun had started breaking through the clouds. He hoped they could pick up the pace and reach the regiment before sunset. As Alexander's horse strode barely a foot into the clearing, lightning struck the earth before them, blinding the three horsemen. Alexander's horse reeled, and he was tossed to the ground. Strangely, the light didn't fade, and what happened next almost broke the man's mind.

The Garden of Scripture

"Jackson," a voice like music and thunder said coming from the direction of the light. "Why do you persecute me?"

A mixture of awe and deep fear surged through Jackson. Surely, he did not hear what he just had, had he? If it were not for the intensity of the light, Jackson would have thought he was dreaming. "What is this? Who are you?" He asked, trembling, with his arm shielding his eyes.

"I am Jesus, whom you are persecuting."

Jackson said nothing in return. In the briefest instant, everything had changed. All his desires, all his firmly held beliefs, and all of his contempt for others.

"Jackson, get up and go to the nearest town, and you will be told what you must do."

The light left, and Jackson could hear the other two men behind him cussing and scrambling to their feet. They, too, listened to the voice but didn't see anyone. The men rushed to his side and helped him up.

"Slowly, please," said Jackson, still trembling. "I . . . I can't see anything. I've been blinded."

"What do you want to do?" The man on his left, Hughes, asked.

"Help me onto my horse. Tie a rope to my saddle's pommel and lead us to the closest town."

The two men looked at each other as if they were conversing silently.

"You really believe that voice?" The man on his right asked.

"I do."

"But," said Hughes, "what if the end of a rope is waiting for you in that town?" he asked. "I've heard about some of the things you've done. Hell, the things I did ain't much better," he said with a forlorn expression.

"Hughes," replied Jackson, heavy with grief. "I feel that he could have me see justice anywhere." His eyes began to fill with tears, and suddenly, the words of a Scripture verse he memorized as a child crashed into him like a runaway wagon. It slipped out of his lips, saying, "And the King shall answer and say unto them,

Verily I say unto you, inasmuch as ye have done it unto one of the least of these my brethren, ye have done it unto me." The tears flowed freely after he spoke those holy words. "Oh, God! What have I done? Please, Hughes, help me on my horse," he wept, his heart wrenching inside of his chest. "Bring me to the town."

They did as he requested.

Gawonii sat by his small campfire just a stone's throw away from the river, cooking the fish he just caught. It was one of those irritating fires where smoke follows a person everywhere, no matter where they move. But he didn't want to move again and figured it would change direction if the breeze picked up again. The smoke must have affected Gawonii more than he thought because some severe drowsiness set in.

As Gawonii rubbed his eyes, he started at the sound of a man walking out of the bushes and into his camp.

"Gawonii," the man said greeting him. His voice was like music and thunder at the same time. He had dark skin like Gawonii, but not Cherokee, and had short hair. He dressed casually, wearing a loose-fitting white shirt and light brown trousers, and was barefoot. The man had a glorious countenance that shone like the stars on a moonless night. Gawonii instantly prostrated himself as soon as he realized who addressed him.

"Peace, Gawonii. Let me eat with you."

Gawonii slowly sat up and expressed a cautious amazement. "Is this really happening?"

"Well, yes. I am hungry." The Man chuckled pleasantly.

Gawonii laughed nervously and prepared the fish as the Creator of that fish sat next to him.

They ate quietly until the Man spoke up. "Gawonii, I have something for you to do."

All at once, Gawonii's insides lurched, and he got gooseflesh. What on earth did he have to offer?

"Anything," he said.

"I believe that you would do anything for me. I need you to travel to the settlement just a few miles north. You know the one. I also need you to look for the man named Jackson Alexander. He's spent the last day in prayer, and I have given him a vision of you coming to him and laying hands on him so he can see again."

Gawonii was deeply troubled; he knew that man's name. "Lord, I've heard about this man from many in my nation. He has treated us with cruelty. His heart has been filled with hatred for us, and he's backed by powerful people who would take this land from my people."

Gawonii's Creator looked at him with a mixture of profound love and pain on his face. When Gawonii looked into Tsisa's eyes, he swore he could hear the deepest waters of the earth moving, roaring over the stone, splitting rocks.

"Go, Gawonii," Tsisa spoke. "For I have chosen him to carry my cause among the Ani-Yunwiya and your cause among his people and their leaders. He will suffer for your sake and for my name's sake."

Gawonii looked down in thought. An owl sounded off nearby, catching his attention, but he saw Tsisa had gone. So, he took a deep breath, put out the fire, and departed.

It took Gawonii a whole day to travel to where Jackson was. The town was small but growing, as they always do. He nervously asked a few people if they might know where Jackson was located. The people mainly tried to avoid him but softened when they heard how well he spoke English. Would they respond better if he started with reciting St. Augustine? Finally, a wheelwright pointed him toward a small building serving as a Methodist chapel.

Gawonii knocked on the door. A short, balding man with wire spectacles, whom he supposed was the chaplain, opened the door and smiled at him. "He's there at the table," the short man said in a deeper voice than expected.

In front of them was Jackson, doubled over a table in trance-like prayer. "He's been fasting since he arrived two days ago," the Chaplain said.

Gawonii looked at Jackon, who barely noticed anyone else in the room. This man, who represented everything Gawonii and his people feared, had tormented them for almost a decade and was rumored to have no remorse for what he did, now appeared so

A Disruptive God

frail. Jackson's frailness, however, didn't drum up any sympathy or love for Gawonii; he'd done too much against them. It would be his love for Tsisa for which he would be laying his hands on this man.

"Jackson," called Gawonii. Jackson, startled, turned in his seat and looked up to search for Gawonii, who thought his eyes looked like a cloudy morning. He took a few steps towards him and obediently yet gently placed his hands on each side of Jackson's face. "Brother Jackon," he said, "the Lord Jesus who appeared to you on the road by which you came has sent me so that you may regain your sight and be filled with the Holy Spirit."

Gawonii gasped when he saw Jackson's cloudy eyes instantly clear, revealing light green irises. Jackson clasped Gawonii's hands, which were still on his face, with his own. As Jackson looked at Gawonii's face, tears began to fill his eyes. He stood up, trembling somewhat.

"You..." Jackson tried to speak. His face became confused and crowned with shame. "You put your hands on me out of love. And I only used my hands to harm your people." He said through sobs.

Gawonii looked away. "I only did it out of love for Christ," he admitted.

"I believe that is enough," Jackson replied with faith.

The statement hit Gawonii like lightning. Jackson was right; it was enough. Somehow, that realization radically changed his view of the man before him. It was as if Tsisa somehow flung the doors open to love others through obediently loving him. Whereas he had called Jackson a brother as a matter of formality only a moment ago, now Jackson was his brother. Gawonii's spirit was deeply moved, and he, too, began to shed tears. "You are right, brother. He is enough."

Standing a few feet away, watching the whole exchange, the Chaplain stepped close to both of them and put a hand on each man's shoulder. "Gentlemen, God has done something new today, but also old. May the grace of God continue to go with you both."

In this anachronistic retelling of the Apostle Paul's conversion story, we see a person, Jackson, whom current society would probably not want to see redeemed because of his gleefully harsh treatment of a less powerful minority group. By most standards, he didn't deserve it. Unlike Andy Dufresne, both Paul and Jackson were guilty of committing dreadful crimes, even if they were legally sanctioned. It would only be fitting if they faced a punishment or end that reflected the ugly things they'd done. Yet, it's the nature of God's grace that always offers redemption to those who don't deserve his or anyone else's favor. If we're honest with ourselves, we can admit that we all do things that can make us unlovable, and we commit them all too willingly. Even so, God continues to work with such flawed beings. But he doesn't leave us rooted in the flaws of our sins. He rescues our unlovable selves and lavishes us with love (Eph 1:7–8). Such favor is both maddening and staggeringly beautiful at the same time. And for people who encounter the redemption that Christ brings, he is enough for them; they don't need to seek it from anyone else or demand anyone notice. Their redemption is on display in the fruit they bear.

DISRUPTIVE NEIGHBORS

Redemption isn't the only disruption that Christ Jesus brings to our lives, and we saw a little bit of another one in the story about Jackson and Gawonii. In the middle of Luke 10, Jesus is welcoming back the seventy disciples he sent out previously to share the gospel, telling them they are blessed for what they have seen and heard because many in Israel's past had longed for the same, but never experienced it (Luke 10:23–24). Suddenly, like in the Spanish Inquisition skit from *Monty Python*, a lawyer pops up to test Jesus, asking him what it takes to inherit eternal life. Jesus knows what's up, though, and turns the question around on the lawyer who answers correctly, "You shall love the Lord your God with all your heart and with all your soul and with all your strength and with all your mind and your neighbor as yourself."

The lawyer is not pleased enough with the test and may not have expected Jesus to flip it around on him. So, he keeps pushing the envelope, asking, "And who is my neighbor?" This question is often viewed as the lawyer just wanting to be a pain; he is trying

A Disruptive God

to test Jesus. Whatever the lawyer's attitude or motive might be, the question he asks is probably one of the most theologically significant questions Jesus is asked in his entire ministry. It would be like someone today asking, "What happened on the cross?" It's so important that Jesus' answer can only be communicated through telling a parable, the parable of the Good Samaritan, saying,

> A man was going down from Jerusalem to Jericho, and he fell among robbers, who stripped him and beat him and departed, leaving him half dead. Now by chance a priest was going down that road, and when he saw him he passed by on the other side. So likewise a Levite, when he came to the place and saw him, passed by on the other side. But a Samaritan, as he journeyed, came to where he was, and when he saw him, he had compassion. He went to him and bound up his wounds, pouring on oil and wine. Then he set him on his own animal and brought him to an inn and took care of him. And the next day he took out two denarii and gave them to the innkeeper, saying, "Take care of him, and whatever more you spend, I will repay you when I come back." (Luke 10:30–35)

To drive the impact of the parable home, Jesus then asks the lawyer, "Which of these three, do you think, proved to be a neighbor to the man who fell among the robbers?" The lawyer then answers that it was obviously the Samaritan, and Jesus then tells him he must be that kind of neighbor.

Jesus thwarts the lawyer in a few ways using the parable. Firstly, one of the purposes of telling a parable is to throw a listener off balance, especially if they're expecting a straightforward answer. This requires the listener to think more critically about the subject they asked about rather than treating the information as "a simple acquisition of facts."[6] Secondly, parables used the medium of stories to reveal biblical truths and could fix themselves in the minds of those who heard them.[7] Those around the lawyer, up to seventy other people, would have remembered the story and

---

6. Anthony and Benson, *Christian Education*, 100.
7. Anthony and Benson, *Christian Education*, 100.

THE GARDEN OF SCRIPTURE

placed the lawyer as the center of attention, including his reaction. Third, Jesus throws the religious contemporaries of the lawyer, such as the priest and the Levite, under the bus. In Jesus' day, not all those who identified themselves as a priest or Levites were trained to be one; many were merely born into priestly families, and that ancestry was what was held in esteem more than their service in the Temple.[8] Still, they were seen as the epitome of piety because of their association with the Temple.

All those disruptions of the inquisitive lawyer acted as a build-up to the largest one. The hero of the story was not a Jew but a Samaritan. To suggest that the Samaritan came to the rescue and not the two "holy men" who passed the half-dead man by, even in a story, would be scandalous to an audience of Jews. Not only were Samaritans considered to be foreigners by Jews, but it's also said that Samaritans rejected the Jerusalem-centered salvation history and worship of God in Jerusalem's temple, which flew in the face of Hebrew Scripture and tradition.[9] Instead, Samaritans centered their worship of God on Mount Gerizim in Samaria. Because of these differences, conflicts often arose between the two groups, such as in 128 BC when a Jewish king destroyed the temple on Mount Gerizim.[10] So, then, to say that not only was the Samaritan the rescuer, but then to also show that he kept outshining the holy men by bandaging the beaten man, bringing him to an inn, and paying for his care, I can only imagine then how high the lawyer's eyebrows must have been raised.

Knowing a bit of the cultural background of the Jews and Samaritans, we can see how Jesus' parable must have dizzied the lawyer. The shocking statements Jesus makes force him to admit that the Samaritan was the true neighbor of the beaten man while also highlighting how the religious elites have failed to show the faithful compassion God desires his people to show. However, even if we can make an educated guess that Jesus' parable of the Good Samaritan embarrassed the lawyer, Jesus doesn't make the

---

8. Green, *The Gospel of Luke*, 479.
9. Green, *The Gospel of Luke*, 479.
10. Keener, *Acts*, 262.

A Disruptive God

embarrassment the lesson, for the lawyer isn't beyond redemption. The lesson for the lawyer is that faithfulness to God requires his followers to show mercy and compassion, which is seen in Jesus' statement to "Go and do likewise" (10:37).

Furthermore, we can't feel too smug about the lawyer's reaction. The reason is that he serves as a surrogate for the audience. If you're unfamiliar with the role, an audience surrogate is a film character representing the viewer. It has been said that the lawyer's question of, "And who is my neighbor?" can also be understood as "Who can I avoid?" The latter question is something humans feel on a fundamental level. There are certain people we wish to not interact with for various reasons, but mainly because we are culturally conditioned to be uncomfortable by their presence. Through Jesus answering the lawyer, he also answers the reader, us. In the strictest possible terms, if we want to be compassionate and merciful rescuers, our neighbors must include the people we consider our enemies. Or worse, the people who really annoy us.

Additionally, it can be said that this parable of the Good Samaritan is not only a nod to God's saving action on humanity's behalf but also what all those rescued by God need to do. We are the beaten man whose sins have appeared to have defeated us. The two "holy men" are the institutions we thought would and should have aided us, perhaps the religious whose love has grown cold. Then God, who, in our sin, we have made an enemy, comes along in Christ and rescues us, bandaging us, anointing us with his healing love, and gives us a place to stay at his own cost (in his case, the price of his blood) and then bringing us to the community of his followers whom he charges with taking care of each other and the broken (Matt 25:35–46). There is also an assumed cost, a disruption, on account of Jesus' community, which helps lift the burdens of others. Indeed, Jesus tells us of this in Luke 14:28. It's all grounded in the *agape* love of God; therefore, it is sacrificial in nature and compels us to be sacrificial. But just as the Samaritan says he will pay the innkeeper upon his return, Jesus promises us the reward of eternity with him (Matt 25:46b), and it is at the cross where we find that Jesus means what he says when he teaches the parable of the Good Samaritan.

The gospels and the Bible are filled with other examples of how God's wisdom disrupts the lives of his followers so that we can be shaped. We must let the Wisdom of God found in Scripture continually disrupt us because the influences of a fallen world with all its temptations never rest. We can't show the maddening yet exceedingly graceful redemption God offers, nor the layered self-sacrificial and enemy-loving nature of God's love if we approach our reading as a mere method of collecting facts and if we don't allow God to "trouble and thwart" the conventional wisdom of the world inside of us.

6

The Cloud

Though we cannot think alike, may we not love alike? May we not be of one heart, though we are not of one opinion? Without all doubt, we may. Herein all the children of God may unite, notwithstanding these smaller differences.[1]

—John Wesley

THE WAR OF THE CRYSTAL

The island of Sarxia was vast. It contained lush vegetation, vibrant animal life, majestic mountain ranges, serene valleys, scenic coastlands, and tranquil rivers and lakes. On the island existed three kingdoms: the Kingdom of the Sun, the Kingdom of the Land, and the Kingdom of the Waters. The three kingdoms showed their devotion to the elements they followed in almost every facet of their respective societies, and each kingdom knew individuals among them who were from other kingdoms based on their clothing. For instance, people from the Sun Kingdom clothed themselves in bright reds, oranges, and yellows. Citizens of the Kingdom of the Land were known for their multi-shaded

---

1. Wesley, "Catholic Spirit," 706.

green and brown garments, and the denizens of the Kingdom of the Waters sported blues, whites, and silvers.

All three kingdoms lived in relative peace with one another. The old writings say the peace was primarily due to the three peoples practicing a similar religion. At the center of each kingdom stood a temple with a giant crystal that glowed with the colors of the kingdom it resided in. As the writings say, wandering mystics traveled the island and testified that all three crystals were once part of a larger one but had been fragmented and separated in a time that was lost to them. Such a belief enabled the three lands to make room for one another and even prompted them to pay tribute to each other for their shared ancestry.

The tranquility lasted for hundreds upon hundreds of years. As long as the people of each kingdom listened to the mystics, the crystals glowed brightly, never fading, and their lands were blessed. A time came, however, when some began ignoring the mystics, which then resulted in the holy teachings dwindling from family to family. Then, men in every kingdom, who were barely familiar with the teachings, rose to power and began suggesting to their people that the crystal housed in their capital cities was the original crystal, and the others were broken off and stolen. Because the mystics were rare in those times, the citizens of all three lands fell under the sway of their corrupt leaders.

Soon, things became dramatically worse when the light of the crystals began to dim. The people became afraid, and rumors grew in each realm that the other two were somehow responsible for the loss of light. Unbeknownst to the Water and Land Kingdoms, the Sun Kingdom prepared for war. They fashioned wickedly shaped blades and designed engines for battle that spewed fire and released such a noxious black smoke that it choked the birds from the air. Suddenly, mystics appeared again in the Sun Kingdom, denouncing the devastating plans of its leaders and reminding the people of the shared ancestry the people of Sarxia had. However, the Sun King and his council were bent on sieging the other crystals at all costs and commanded the mystics to be put to death.

The Cloud

The Sun Kingdom marched out of their cities and first made for the Kingdom of the Land. Within days of bringing war to the gates of the unassuming opponents, the Sun Kingdom was victorious and captured all inhabitants. Before putting their leaders to the sword, the Sun King publicly ridiculed and humiliated the leaders of the Land Kingdom. Then, they put an end to the temple priests and the men, women, children, and all the beasts of burden that belonged to the Land Kingdom. However, they plundered valuable goods, prized gems, and took possession of their crystal, now only glowing a faint golden-green. Finally, as a hallmark of their victory, the Sun Kingdom burned the cities and villages to ashes.

The Kingdom of the Waters was next. Although the two kingdoms were the opposite in elements, the people of the Waters still fell, as water could not be harnessed like fire. The Sun King repeated the same humiliation and gave the same command of conquest as he did with the Kingdom of the Land. When all had been done, the Sun King took possession of the crystal belonging to the Kingdom of the Waters. In all, the total conquest only took several weeks.

When the Sun King and his army returned to their capital cities, he ordered the priests to bring the two captured crystals to the temple and begin efforts to rejoin them. In a ceremony, the priests located the fracture points and then aligned the crystals so that they appeared to be restored into one whole crystal. The priests and onlookers expected it to glow a fiery red as soon as the pieces were placed. The crystal fused back together as they watched, shining so radiantly that it blinded almost everyone. When the light faded some, those in attendance, including the Sun King, marveled at how the restored crystal shone with a swirling opalescent brilliance. Then, all of them started bowing and worshipping the crystal fervently. Shockingly, a voice emanated from the crystal.

"People of the Sun, what have you done?"

The people were awed and terrified at the voice, which sounded like music and thunder. Then, the Sun King finally spoke up.

"God of gods, we, your true people, have restored you so you can rule over us."

"You have only let jealousy and pride rule over you. The blood of your brothers and sisters stains your hands and cries out from the ground against you. Did you not listen to the mystics I sent to be among you?"

When they heard the voice from the crystal speak those words, all in attendance fell to their knees and wept bitterly. They tore their clothes, and the kingdom became one of wailing rather than victory.

PUTTING DOWN ROOTS

For a long time, I considered myself a wanderer. It might stem from the fact that my family and I took many road trips as a child, often traveling back and forth to Massachusetts every summer and occasionally visiting the Southwestern part of the United States. In my early twenties, I made several moves all between Minnesota, Massachusetts, and western New York. When I met my wife, I moved to Georgia to be with her, although we attempted a brief stint in Massachusetts. Picking up and leaving became commonplace, and I began to prefer it. Even several years into living in Georgia, I jumped at the chance to move across the country for a ministry opportunity in Oregon.

For the most part, my wife understood my wandering habits. But as we started to add children to the family, Anna expressed that she wanted to root ourselves in the community we already lived in. This was a challenge for me because I always saw us somewhere else. Admittedly, my preferences kept me from making friends and connecting with local ministers. Later on, I did get into ministry leadership for a time, and when I started teaching, I made connections with people that changed my life; I found a community.

THE HISTORICAL ROLE OF COMMUNITY

We are promised to have and be part of a community in the Bible. Many readers believe the first community was Adam and Eve, and they are partly right; those two are the first human ones. However, the first chapter of Genesis reveals that community began with Godself when the words "let us make humankind in our image, according to our likeness" (Gen 1:26). This corresponds with the orthodox doctrine of the Trinity, which states that God is three-in-one, the Father, Son, and Holy Spirit. Therefore, part of being made in the image of God is to exist with others in a community. But that's not all; the creation account of Genesis 2 reveals another community before humanity when it says, "These are the generations of the heavens and the earth" (2:4). So, with the Trinity, humanity and even the other aspects of creation, that makes three visible communities within just the first two pages of the Bible.

Things went horribly wrong, though, when Adam and Eve chose to follow their wisdom over God's. As a result, the harmonious community they once had with God fractured (3:6–24). They were expelled from Eden, and their sin ended up corrupting their children, with one son killing the other (4:8).

But the Bible is a story of how God repairs the communion we once had with him. He starts this by electing Abraham to be the patriarch of a people, Israel, who were meant to bless the nations of the earth (12:1–3). Even though Israel wouldn't keep up with their end of the covenant, God used the lineage of David, their most revered king, to bring forth the Messiah, Jesus, who would redeem humanity and provide the way for people to restore their union with God (John 3:16). Through Jesus' redemptive acts, a new community was born, one that would not only heal Israel's relationship with God but also the divide between Jews and non-Jews (Gal 3:28).

The last two thousand years of the church's history of creating and sustaining community have been a mixed bag. When flesh and blood families savage each other, the church has often been there to bandage them back up and give them a beautiful picture of what it means to be adopted into the family of God. At the same time, the church has harmed itself to the point of division because humans are predictable and complex. For example, in 1054, an event called The Great Schism occurred where the Western part of the church separated from the Eastern part,[2] effectively creating Roman Catholicism and the Eastern Orthodox Church. And then, in 1517, a group known as the Protestants broke away from the Roman Catholic Church when Martin Luther brought forth his list of severe criticisms in Wittenburg, Germany. This action inspired many armed conflicts, resulting in a tremendous amount of bloodshed between members who claimed to worship the same God. Since then, Protestantism has splintered into several thousand denominations, many because of disagreement and others through church planting and missions. Interspersed with all the conflict, however, are plenty of stories of people coming to faith and participating in the new community they find in the church.

These church communities, which make up the body of Christ, are formative. Part of the formative process in the body of Christ has to do with how Scripture is read and understood. Indeed, it is so formative that we can most likely say the issues that arose in the church that caused separation are mainly due to how Scripture was read and understood. The community's formative role in understanding the Bible can happen in a few ways. The most predominant way is established by the denomination. For example, if a local church is part of a Reformed denomination, church members will likely understand the death of Christ through the Penal Substitutionary view of atonement. Or if the church is part of a Pentecostal denomination, the members will hold that the Holy Spirit is still dispensing charismatic gifts as he did with the early church. Finally, let's say someone is a Roman Catholic; their local parish will view that the elements in the Lord's Supper are transformed into the actual body and blood of Christ, a view called Transubstantiation. Each of these three parts views Scripture differently in some way, both significant and insignificant, and will pass on their views through the communal interaction of their congregations.

A second way the church community can influence Bible comprehension is through congregational leadership. Local

---

2. When I say Western and Eastern, it refers to the lands that were once considered the Western and Eastern parts of the Roman Empire.

churches employing the biblical offices of elders and deacons are often placed in leading Bible studies and other types of theological education. More often than not, these leaders hold to the official statements of faith in their denominations. However, because of their position in the church, they may be allowed to insert their own deeply held opinions on what they're teaching based on whatever else they may have studied, which can be a double-edged sword.

Finally, the local church community can impact the understanding of Scripture on the purely lay level through the giving of Testimony. According to authors such as Karen Swallow Prior, who devotes a chapter to the practice in her book *The Evangelical Imagination*, a testimony tells of a person's "conversion story" and often consists of a dramatic transformation highlighting the individual's before and after states of life in Christ.[3] Prior notes, however, that genuine conversion changes how a Christian sees everything and allows a believer's life to be filled with other testimonies about what God has done for them.[4] The testimony's purpose is to showcase the reality of the Gospel's power, the glorification of Christ, and the work of the Holy Spirit.[5] It is a living demonstration or interpretation of Scripture and has the potential for producing good results in evangelizing and the edification of the church.

Some question if testimonies are a valid form of expressing biblical truths. The conversion stories appeal to emotions and experience rather than reason or scriptural exegesis. This is not something that should be dismissed, and Prior brings up a cautionary tale of how a person she once called a friend fabricated a bunch of details in their conversion testimony.[6] Indeed, the practice of telling of one's conversion is so prevalent in Evangelicalism and Pentecostalism that we tend to celebritize the person with the best testimony; this has only increased with social media.

3. Prior, *The Evangelical Imagination*, 85.
4. Prior, *The Evangelical Imagination*, 85.
5. These are my categories based on the witness of many faithful saints.
6. Prior, *The Evangelical Imagination*, 79.

The Garden of Scripture

Nevertheless, testifying to how God has changed our lives has been part of the church almost since its inception; therefore, if we ground the sharing of testimony in the criteria of the Gospel's power, the glorification of Christ, and the work of the Holy Spirit, it can be a formational method of biblical interpretation that is faithful to God's Word.

So, what are we to make of all this? Although no branch, denomination, or Christian community is perfect, we can think of it all, as the author of Hebrews calls it, the great cloud of witness. The cloud consists of people who, in good and bad ways, taught us something valuable about not only what the Bible teaches but how it can and how it shouldn't be lived out.

We should also think of the people who came before us as people who've planted a garden so that the later generations can enjoy what has grown. It is sort of like the home I live in now. The former owners planted red roses, white garden roses, a clematis vine, azalea bushes, and hydrangeas before we moved in. Now, my family enjoys seeing all of them bloom each year. That doesn't mean, however, that my family doesn't bear any responsibility. If we want to see the plants flourish, my wife and I must attend to them to ensure they're healthy and prune them so they don't get out of control. Likewise, the current church must attend to the valuable thoughts and practices of the historical church, thoroughly examining them to understand them better so that we can understand God's Word better and prayerfully prune what might lead us off the rails.

BROADENING OUR DEFINITION OF COMMUNITY

We must also prevent our proverbial "cloud of witness," in the sense of the church, from forming into a thundercloud. In a regular thunderstorm, various types of precipitation collide with one another. The resulting friction causes parts of the thunderclouds to become positively and negatively charged. Lighting then lashes out from the cloud when the differences between the charges become too great, and depending on where it touches, it can wreak

The Cloud

havoc. We have seen such imagery metaphorically play out within the church's history over the result of clashing interpretations of Scripture. It is true that, as the ones charged to go out and make disciples, we must be as responsible as possible to know and say what the Bible says. Still, we must also understand while the Bible is seen as inerrant and infallible by many, no community's interpretation is inerrant and infallible.

Even so, many parts of the cloud of great witness are stormy. The rift between many churchgoers and seminaries is one of the saddest storms. This, no doubt, stems from major Universities that had seminaries adopting the German higher criticism methods of the late nineteenth and early twentieth century. There is a complex history of that movement and the fundamentalism it helped produce. In its most basic sense, the German higher critical method reduced the Bible to being a collection of books of a superstitious culture trying to understand its place in the world. Therefore, while some admired the Bible for Christ's moral teachings, Hebrew and Christian Scriptures lost a lot of authority in the minds of many intellectuals. The result was said to have led to a lot of people deconstructing and losing their faith if they went to seminary and that local churches and large denominations becoming theologically "liberal," meaning they no longer taught core doctrines of Christianity as fundamental truths but stressed they were symbolic of "spiritual truths."

In turn, the numerous evangelical movements still holding to the authority of Scripture, especially in the United States, started their own seminaries. Yet, many conservative Christians who lost trust in those institutions, including pastors, rejected higher education altogether, even if those colleges and seminaries aligned with conservative Christian denominations. This is still the case today, unfortunately. So, some of these Christians may express that *only* the Holy Spirit is needed to understand the Bible.

In chapter 2, I argued that God wants us to understand what he is revealing to us in Scripture and will help us through the Holy Spirit's witness, and I supported it by appealing to both the gospel of John and First Corinthians. We must be careful of limiting how the Spirit will accomplish that understanding to come as if we are the ones in charge. Consider that God "himself granted that some are Apostles, prophets, evangelists, pastors and *teachers* to equip the saints for the work of ministry, for building up the body of Christ" (Eph 4:11–12, emphasis mine). This passage allows us to look at Christian higher education and scholarship differently. We can look at them as provisions of God's grace to the global and historical body of Christ. There are certainly teachers within the body of Christ who have no formal education and are competent; no one is here to argue otherwise. However, teachers who are worth their salt love learning and equally love disseminating and curating what they learn to others. Therefore, the Spirit has led many saints to expand their God-given calling in the university and seminary to develop their potential by studying the languages, cultural backgrounds, and history of the societies represented in the Bible. What Christians who reject higher education might misunderstand is that for the Christian educator and scholar, learning is a spiritual discipline that expresses God's grace, but it isn't the goal. God, and a deepening knowledge of him, is the goal. Similarly, and ironically, the scholars some Christians reject often have a hand translating the Bible those people are reading. Scholars, however, would do well to agree with George MacDonald that no book (in this case, a textbook) is more important than a person.

All this is to say that the Holy Spirit has revealed himself to be multifaceted in illuminating Scripture. The Spirit will illuminate Scripture through individual study, as well as through commentaries and books discussing biblical themes because those scholars and authors are part of the body of Christ. They are in the community of God's people and are working *for* God's people.

We can say the same with the biblical readings that cultures of other ethnicities offer. Christianity was never meant to stay local but range the communities reaching the ends of the earth (Acts 1:8). Since God means to interact with all cultures and ethnicities, those who have interacted with God through the revelation of Scripture will no doubt offer their perspectives. We owe it to ourselves to engage with those readings, especially if they faithfully direct themselves toward God, so we can be genuinely united in Christ. It's dangerous, then, to vilify a believer just because they have a PhD at the end of their name or who represents a different cultural community, and who has put their life's work into a niche part of a biblical field as it may mean being in risk of quenching the work of the Spirit.

When we quench the Spirit, the truth becomes hard to see, love grows cold, and disunity sprouts up in their place. Disunity in a body causes illness, but in a spiritual body like the church, it also causes pride, which can manifest in ugly ways. If they are not careful, soon after, those communities start claiming that *only* their interpretation methods are the correct ones and *only* they are the true church. This has repeatedly happened to the point where an outsider might ask, who has the right God?

We saw the danger of that question play out in the short story at the beginning of this chapter. Denominations within the body of Christ may not become physically violent about correct biblical interpretation these days (that I know of). But there is plenty of character assassination that lends itself to the fracturing of the global body of Christ. Just look on social media for evidence.

But what of our cloud of witness? In the book of Hebrews, the author uses the metaphor to suggest that those who took hold of God's promises in the Old Testament were looking upon those who experienced Christ and were now part of his church.[7] In many ways, their hope in the promised Messiah and his kingdom propelled the community of Israel forward. The cloud also represents the shekinah glory of God, his divine presence, which descended on Mt. Sinai and the Tabernacle in the wilderness after the Israelites fled Egypt.[8] Therefore, the people of the past who make up that cloud are witnessing the audience of Hebrews from the position of God's divine presence; they are *with* God. So, too, are we present believers with God since Christ's title of Emmanuel is God with us. God's Spirit also dwells within the hearts of Christians, which means we are enabled to reflect the glory of God.

7. Gause, *Hebrews*, 297
8. Gause, *Hebrews*, 297.

The Garden of Scripture

Therefore, when we read and come across readings of Scripture that may differ from our own, we need to remember how others may bring glory to God and if our response matches a character that brings glory to God.

To consider this further, we can look at what the Apostle Paul writes in Colossians:

> Therefore, as God's chosen ones, holy and beloved, clothe yourselves with compassion, kindness, humility, meekness, and patience. Bear with one another and, if anyone has a complaint against another, forgive each other; just as the Lord has forgiven you, so you also must forgive. Above all, clothe yourselves with love, which binds everything together in perfect harmony. And let the peace of Christ rule in your hearts, to which indeed you were called in one body. And be thankful. Let the word of Christ dwell in you richly; teach and admonish one another in all wisdom; and with gratitude in your hearts sing psalms, hymns, and spiritual songs to God. And whatever you do, in word or deed, do everything in the name of the Lord Jesus, giving thanks to God the Father through him. (Col 3:12–17)

This passage provides a good litmus test for how we interpret the Bible and communicate our interpretation and how we view others' interpretation and interact with them in the community of Christ. We can ask, am I clothing myself in the virtues of Christ? Am I quick to forgive and genuine when I ask for forgiveness? Do I clothe myself in such a love that binds us together? Do I truly let the peace of Christ, which has overcome the world (John 16:33), rule within me in a way that unites me with others? Do I show gratitude for the people in my life and the people God uses to help me grow? Do I abide in Christ and let him abide in me to the point where his wisdom and the wisdom of Scripture overflow out of me and into the lives of those around me? Do I respond to the critiques or perspectives of different people with that wisdom? Lastly, have I devoted every corner of my being to Christ, who in turn forms me into a person who inhabits all of the traits above, which pleases God?

THE CLOUD

The above can be difficult questions to confront ourselves with sometimes. They, and the passage they derive from, however, point to how the entire New Testament after the gospels views what it's like to be a community with its foundation in Christ. Writers such as Paul, Peter, Jude, and even Luke (in Acts) only speak negatively of people in the community when those people purposely teach or lead people in a way that is consistent with the fallen order of the world or try to add extra steps beyond having faith in Christ and being obedient to him (1 Cor 11:17–22, 30, Gal 1:6–8, 3:14, 2 Tim 3:1–13, 2 Peter 2, 3 John 1:9–10, Jude 1:3–19). However, the writers believed, especially Paul, that being part of the community was uniting all who belonged.

A HALF-WAY FUNCTIONING CLOUD

Conversely, just because we read and apply those passages in how we approach the community locally and globally doesn't mean everything will be rainbows and butterflies. In this book, *The Community of God*, Doug Bursch conveys that we too easily buy into a utopian vision of Christianity.[9] A utopia is a state of existence where the community runs as it should, with everything striking the right balance, where every need is met, and everyone has recognized value collectively and individually.[10] Bursch says that as a young pastor, he bought into a utopian ideal, believing that he could guide his congregants into a community free of conflict if he just said and did the right things.[11] Bursch reminds us that a utopia, a place or community without any conflict, can't exist because the word utopia is a Greek word meaning "no such place."[12] Conflict is part of the church's life, a product of diverse "differents" and "sames" coming into contact. Strife even existed among Jesus and his disciples as they argued who among them was the greatest

---

9. Bursch, *The Community of God*, 3.
10. Bursch, *The Community of God*, 3.
11. Bursch, *The Community of God*, 6.
12. Bursch, *The Community of God*, 4.

and when Jesus rebuked Peter. Let us not forget about how Judas Iscariot betrayed Jesus. Profoundly beautiful things can happen in a church community and the global body of believers, but so can the polar opposite. And we ourselves will sometimes fail at being gracious and loving neighbors. Sometimes, we will even trick ourselves into thinking we've failed. Yet God may use those apparent and unintended failings to surprise us with something *good* as if we're failing upward.

Nevertheless, it is the inspired truth of the New Testament writers that says the kind of soul-crushing conflict we experience in a fallen world can be significantly reduced in the life of the church if we keep in step with the Spirit, yielding ourselves to how he is forming us, and keep our eyes on the object of our worship, Christ Jesus. So, be wary of the voices who'd try to restrict you when searching for the meanings of difficult Scripture passages. Be cautious of those who are constantly criticizing Christian sisters and brothers who are outside their own traditions. Be careful of those who are continually attacking Christian scholars and be wary of those who imply that only their tradition correctly interprets Scripture, for that is what the ancient Gnostics used to claim. While we want to be as responsible as possible when interpreting what the Bible says beyond the surface level, no "one" person or denomination is the final authority on the authority of Scripture. Our local community is a help to us, but the whole Christian community is just as a powerful witness. We would be fooling and possibly harming ourselves if we thought we didn't need their wisdom. We are not in this alone, but together.

7

Behold The Man!

The birth, death and resurrection of Jesus means that one day everything sad will come untrue.

—J. R. R. Tolkien

When I finished seminary, I had many grand ideas of what I wanted to accomplish next. Even though my degree was beneficial for teaching, I had this notion that I'd somehow be able to secure a job as an adjunct instructor at a Christian college. I also wanted to travel overseas and attend theological and ecumenical conferences. Last but not least, I wanted to pastor. One out of three of those things came to pass; I did end up on a church staff pastoring for a time. The other two didn't happen, mostly because I needed more schooling and connections. Those dashed dreams left me without a career, and although I had an income, I was left unfulfilled.

One day, however, my wife told me about a position at a private Christian school that had opened up and needed a K–8th grade Bible and Social studies teacher. A humbler person probably would have jumped at the opportunity, but I initially dismissed it because I didn't want to work with that age range. One reason for that was my having served in children's ministry for three years in the church my family attended. The other reason was that I thought I was above teaching those ages. I wanted to teach older students and get into the more complicated and nuanced aspects of the Christian faith. I had the naïve belief that age equals maturity. I got over my pride quickly, though, when my wife gave me "the look." So, I applied and took the position when it was offered.

I can say that on my first day of teaching, my students humbled me very quickly. Teaching K–8th grade every day rather than just on Sundays taught me that if I couldn't teach them what I knew in a way they would understand, I probably wouldn't be able to teach anyone very well. The other thing I quickly recognized was that children are often overlooked as part of the church. We usually describe the youngest generation as the future of the church, but that isn't true. Yes, adults might be able to comprehend more profound theological truths and even be able to step into ministry leadership, but those two things aren't a qualifier for being part of the body of Christ; following Jesus is, and plenty of kids do follow him. It was from the experiences of teaching young students daily that I discovered a fountain of purpose and fulfillment, way more than I could have comprehended before I took the position.

In the first century, Israel faced a similar scenario where the idea and the expectation of the Messiah were concerned, but obviously on a much more profound scale. Contrary to what some may believe, Israel didn't have a monolithic view of what or who the Messiah was. This was mainly due to the variety of thought within "intertestamental Judaism," the period between the last Old and the first New Testament writings. (It must be noted that although about four hundred years passed, it didn't mean the Jewish people stopped writing.) Some in Israel didn't even think the title would belong to an individual but perhaps to the nation of Israel itself; there were also schools of thought that believed there would be several Messiahs.[1]

Even though the ordinary people and the Pharisees had somewhat of a shared vision of the Messiah as an individual, there was

---

1. Scott Jr., *Jewish Backgrounds*, 308–10.

diversity in thought concerning his function.² For example, while many maintained that a messianic figure would be from the line of King David, many from the tribe of Levi hoped the Messiah would come from their circles.³ Such a hope would shift the paradigm of the Messiah from a purely political function, who would deliver Israel to national independence, to a priestly yet kingly function since the Levites were in charge of Temple worship. The Israelites wanted to be the religious powerhouse they were once meant to become. Additionally, the titles of the Messiah, such as the Son of Man, the Servant of the Lord, the Prophet like Moses, and even Elijah, could have been seen as separate individuals rather than titles by which one figure would be known.⁴

It seems, then, that many of the Jews in Israel and even abroad had a wide range of wishes of how the Messiah would look and function. Instead of forming a general consensus, it also appeared to cause confusion and probably some tension between the differing factions. However, it is clear that they were all looking for a savior, and the one they got didn't meet their wishes but went wildly beyond them to a place where their most profound needs were met. That makes Jesus dangerous. Though many have tried, we can't control him or his image. However, that uncontrollableness is also what makes him so wonderous.

JESUS, KING OF THE COSMOS

John's gospel gives us a stunning picture of why Christ is uncontrollable. At the end of his gospel, John writes a truly fascinating sentence, saying, "But there are also many other things that Jesus did; if everyone of them were written down, I suppose that the world itself could not contain the books that would be written" (John 21:25). There are many reasons why it might be fascinating. But for me, it's because they seem to be the words of a true

---

2. Scott Jr., *Jewish Backgrounds*, 308–10.
3. Scott Jr., *Jewish Backgrounds*, 311
4. Scott Jr., *Jewish Backgrounds*, 309.

storyteller in the sense that he is telling a true story and that the author is masterful. John doesn't limit the focus of his writing, Jesus, while admitting that the rest of what Jesus does is not up to him because he lives beyond the pen or the quill.

However, part of John's sentence raises a question to muse on. When he says, "But there are also many other things that Jesus did," does he mean it in terms of Jesus' earthly ministry or something else? There is an easy answer; it is John acknowledging the importance of the other gospels. After all, they contain events in Jesus' life that do not appear in his gospel account. Luke, specifically, even offers stories from Jesus' childhood, such as when Mary and Joseph brought him to the Temple and interacted with Anna and Simeon and when Jesus stayed behind at the Temple as a twelve-year-old. The other easy answer is to recognize that one's entire life, like what time a person brushes their teeth every day and how long it takes, wouldn't be able to fit in a single book, not even twenty-seven books.

Because the gospels focus so much on Jesus' earthly ministry, it can be challenging to remember that Christ was in action long before his incarnation. That's understandable, given this world is all we know; we are intrinsically tied to this earth, and we encounter our surroundings primarily through our physical senses and don't typically think about what's happening outside of them.

Perhaps John's ending sentence should be considered in light of his opening sentences, stating, "In the beginning was the Word, and the Word was with God, and the Word was God. He was in the beginning with God" (John 1:1–2). These verses help us ponder that Jesus is not the typical person. Jesus is *the* Person, the second Person of the Trinity. Before he descended from the heavens to be incarnated and born of a virgin named Mary, he was pre-existent with the Father and Holy Spirit. Those verses, in fact, intentionally mirror the first words of Genesis. John also sees Christ as an equal if not primary force in creation, writing, "All things came into being through him, and without him, not one thing came into being" (1:3). This is Christ operating as the *Logos;* a term communicating the creative power and wisdom of God in ancient Hebrew thought.

Wisdom was not just seen as a trait, but it is spoken of as almost a supernatural and supreme individual. "The LORD possessed me at the beginning of his work," says the writer of Proverbs 8, channeling Wisdom, "the first of his acts of old" (Prov 8:22). He then goes on to say that Wisdom was "beside him [Yahweh], like a master workman, and I was daily his delight, rejoicing before him always" (8:30).

Other writers in the New Testament confirm John's view of Jesus as the pre-existent Christ who reigned over the universe. In Colossians, the Apostle Paul tells his audience, "For in him all things in heaven and on earth were created, things visible and invisible, whether thrones or dominions or rulers or powers—all things have been created through him and for him" (Col 1:16). The same goes for the author of Hebrews, who says, "By faith we understand that the worlds were prepared by the *word* of God, so that what is seen was made from things that are not visible" (Heb 11:3, emphasis mine).[5] John's opening, which stresses Jesus' divine nature, is one of the reasons why his gospel is so important. It shows us that the spiritual world is irrevocably linked with the physical and that, perhaps, we think about the spiritual wrongly. It is less about what goes bump in the dark, crystal balls, and Ouija boards, and more about how God permeates and is active in all of existence; every space, even the unseen space, is filled with the presence of God and is being reconciled to him. Without John's reminder that Jesus is truly God, we would miss out on a critical aspect of Jesus's role as Messiah, that he is God in the flesh who reconciles us back to God's self and that Jesus shows just how far God is willing to humiliate himself to save us.

Here, again, as in chapter 4, we come to swimming in the fullness of God. Seeing Jesus as having existed for eternity means there'll never be a time that we're without Jesus, even if there was a time when he hadn't been revealed. Thus, Jesus, in Revelation, can call himself the Alpha and Omega (Rev 1:8). All history was

---

5. Gause, *Hebrews*, 255. Gause contends that based on the linguistic evidence in Hebrews and the book's overarching high Christology, that "word" (*rhema*) is meant to be understood as the word of Christ.

leading up to him, and the rest of history continuing into eternity will come back around to him. The Bible, then, is essentially a witness to how salvation history revolves around Christ as he "came to what was his own" (John 1:11). Jesus confirms this very notion when he confronts the Pharisees, saying, "You search the scriptures because you think that in them you have eternal life, and it is they that testify on my behalf" (John 5:39).

THE GOOD KIND OF FOOLISHNESS

Now, we come to the humanity of Jesus. Some may be asking if Christ was pre-existent, co-ruled, and created with the Father, would it not be enough for him to save the world as he was? That is a perfectly valid question. The idea that an all-powerful being who rules the universe and then who would Incarnate himself into a fully human person seems somewhat unnecessary and even foolish. If, in your struggle to comprehend the Holy Scriptures, you've struggled with the humanity of Christ, I'm giving you permission to think it foolish or feel foolish yourself.

However, I also want you to know that it seems foolish because it goes against the conventional wisdom we're raised in. Conventional wisdom is any belief that is a generally accepted theory or belief the surrounding culture holds. Every society throughout the Earth's history has been steeped in its own wisdom, which, we can safely say, goes unquestioned most of the time. The Apostle Paul and the New Testament writers often faced off against the conventional wisdom of his day. For Paul, though, this "foolishness" of the gospel, which rests on Jesus' life, crucifixion, and resurrection, is meant to upend the wisdom of the world (1 Cor 1:18–25).

Furthermore, it must be understood that our cultures often structure things around conventional wisdom; the beliefs in them are normative. Conventional wisdom can be understood with simple and innocuous statements like "the early bird gets the worm," which tries to offer simple yet helpful advice. But it can and often does make a hard turn towards deeply held and treacherous sentiments like "God will never give you more than you can handle" and "so-and-so is our only chance at turning this country around." So, conventional wisdom may be genuinely held to be accurate, and beliefs may even be forced by some individuals and groups to be true. Either way, this type of wisdom doesn't leave much room for diving under the surface of essential matters.

In trying to understand the message of the Gospel (or, in this case, specifically, the humanity of Christ) through those norms, we become like the characters Pintel and Ragetti from the *Pirates of the Caribbean* movie franchise. In the third film, *At World's End*, the crew of the Black Pearl, of which the two are a part, manages to rescue Jack Sparrow from the underworld. However, for the crew to return to the living world, they must capsize the Black Pearl at a specific time after sunset. So, while everyone is running from side to side of the ship to capsize it, Pintel and Ragetti tie themselves upside down to the mast after they convince themselves they'll be right side up when the Pearl returns to the land of the living. They soon realize, however, that their wisdom has led them to miscalculate their strategy. Upon their return to the world of living, they still find themselves tied upside down and looking like fools.

It was this way for many who came in contact with the Gospel in the ancient world. Paul mentions that the Greeks wanted to understand God through their own systems of wisdom and philosophy and that the Jewish leaders wanted God to reveal himself through signs because, for the Jews, that is how God revealed himself in the past (1:22). There was, for example, a heretical community of Christians called the Docetists whose hard held beliefs kept them from grasping the humanity of Jesus and over-emphasized his divinity. Docetists believed that Jesus only appeared to be human so that his divinity was not compromised.[6] This belief most likely stemmed from Greek philosophy, which considered humanity a dualistic form of body and soul.[7] The soul was believed by the ancient Greeks to be immortal, and the body was what housed it; some even said it was imprisoned by the body.[8] Because the Greeks

---

6. Culpepper, *The Gospel and Letters of John*, 51.
7. Lane, *History of Christian Thought*, 7.
8. Lane, *History of Christian Thought*, 7.

despised the material world for its changing nature, the body was seen negatively, consisting of corruptible physical matter.[9] Although, like Christians, many Greek thinkers recognized a need for salvation, the thought of a Supreme God manifesting himself into a human body and even dying would have wholly contradicted their beliefs.[10] Since God fully reveals himself through Jesus, which includes his full humanity, they end up stumbling over it, not matching their conventional wisdom. They cast it off as foolishness, and it caused them to fracture within some Christian communities, leading the Apostle John to write, "And the Word became flesh and lived among" us (John 1:14).

God means to turn the world on its head with his wisdom. Those seeking him find themselves upright as they are saved by his foolishness, while the others who refuse to accept God's wisdom, like the Docetists, will find themselves upside down. So, it's okay to see the Gospel and the idea that God would become man as foolish or feel foolish for believing in it, but the reward for that foolishness is gaining union with God and his wisdom.

Jesus' humanity is a crucial part of the atonement. Although his sacrifice on the cross can't and shouldn't be understated, the fact of the matter is that Christ's redeeming work began with his birth, what is referred to as the Incarnation. The Incarnation is sometimes only treated as a condition in which Jesus was able to redeem humanity, but that is a limited view. Instead, the Incarnation becomes more potent if we consider it to be the action of the Word (the Logos) embracing the fullness of the human experience.[11] That is why the author of Hebrews can say, "he had to become like his brothers and sisters in every respect" (Heb 2:17a).

The exception, of course, is that Jesus didn't embrace sin. Yet, by embracing humanity and possessing it all, he can redeem it all.[12]

    9. Lane, *History of Christian Thought*, 7..
    10. Lane, *History of Christian Thought*, 7.
    11. Reardon, *Reclaiming the Atonement*, 21.
    12. Reardon argues this redemption reached the practices of "history, philosophy, language, literature, and psychology," since those fields are expressions of humanity and "bear man's intrinsic capacity for spiritual transformation."

Just as the crucifixion can't be understated, it can't be understated that in the Incarnation, Jesus assumed "a soul, mind, and a will—everything that is human,"[13] so that, as one medieval theologian put it, "In order to be united to the whole of our nature in order to penetrate and assimilate us into Himself by totally uniting what is proper to Him with what is proper to us."[14]

In concert with Jesus' full humanity redeeming our whole human selves, the Incarnation is a profound statement that God's creation of man and woman is part of his *good* creation. We are told in the first chapter of Genesis that humans are created in the image of God. With that title, we were given royal authority to co-rule with God over what he created. In the second chapter of Genesis, humanity is charged with the priestly role of caring for and cultivating creation. Then, in Genesis 3, we can gather when it says, "the Lord God walking in the garden at the time of the evening breeze," as Adam and Eve have an intimate relationship with God. Although their relationship and image-bearing are marred by choosing to rule by their own wisdom rather than God's, and heavy consequences ensue, God doesn't abandon them. Even when God, later on, despairs over creating humanity and judges them with a catastrophic flood (Gen 6:6–7), the fact that he finds a righteous man in Noah and his family, sparing them and making a covenant with them signifies that God means to keep his own word of humanity being a *good* part of creation.

KING JESUS

God keeps his word through Jesus. Through the Incarnation, Jesus doesn't just embrace full humanity, but he takes on and redeems humanity's royal and priestly roles. Our Lord can do this not because he was made in the image of God but because "He is the

---

See Reardon, *Reclaiming the Atonement*, 21."

13. Reardon, *Reclaiming the Atonement*, 54.

14. Cabasilas, *The Life in Christ* 4.6. As quoted in Reardon, *Reclaiming the Atonement*, 54. Cabasilas was primarily referring to what happens in the sacrament of the Lord's Supper, but I think it fits well with this too.

image of the invisible God" (Col 1:15). With the section on the pre-existent Christ, it is easy to see the royal role of Christ. We can also see Jesus' rule over creation through the miracles and healings he performed. However, it should be noted that Jesus' complete faithfulness to his Father's will, even going to death, signifies the faithfulness to God that Adam and Eve should have maintained in the beginning. After his resurrection, he expects those faithful to him to be as faithful as he was. As a king would command his subject, Jesus tells his disciples:

> All authority in heaven and on earth has been given to me. Go therefore and make disciples of all nations, baptizing them in the name of the Father and of the Son and of the Holy Spirit and teaching them to obey everything that I have commanded you. And remember, I am with you always, to the end of the age. (Matt 28:18–20)

On the other hand, Jesus' rulership had already been displayed in different ways. If choosing to rule by our own wisdom fractured our relationship with God, then only a life infused with the love of choosing God's wisdom can prepare the rest of humanity for his coming kingdom. Jesus was such a man. We can see this in Matthew's portrayal of the Sermon on the Mount. The sermon, which comprises three chapters (5–7) in the gospel of Matthew, gets to the core of raw humanity. The late Dallas Willard, in his fantastic book *The Divine Conspiracy*, suggests the sermon touches on two fundamental questions that speak to the religious context of Israel. The first one, though, is a very human one: which life is the good life?[15] This touches upon another inherent question, "What is genuinely in my interest and how may I enter true well-being?"[16] The second main question is, "Who has the kind of goodness found in God himself, constituting the family likeness between God and his children?"[17]

---

15. Williard, *The Divine Conspiracy*, 111.
16. Williard, *The Divine Conspiracy*, 111.
17. Williard, *The Divine Conspiracy*, 111.

Although Jesus' answers to these questions are in keeping with the Torah and the prophets, the teachings in those two have been implemented by religious leaders who suffer from faulty wisdom. For example, the people thought to be blessed were those who appeared to be righteous by reputation, like the Pharisees, the Temple priests, and the wealthy, since wealth was seen as coming from God's favor. However, when Jesus says things like "blessed are those who are poor in spirit, for theirs is the kingdom of heaven" (Matt 5:3), he is proclaiming that the people who fell through the religious cracks, the spiritual zeroes, as Willard says—people who can't make heads or tails of religion but who still fill the pews—also have a place in the kingdom of God.[18] And indeed, Jesus had just ministered to those people at the close of Matthew's fourth chapter. The "spiritual zeroes" have access to the kingdom because Jesus is the one bringing the kingdom of God and also because they are created in the image of God.

Jesus spends the remaining bulk of the sermon, roughly 5:17–7:12, addressing the second question, "Who has the kind of goodness found in God himself, constituting the family likeness between God and his children?" The answer to this question is found in righteousness. The word righteousness can mean a lot of things to a lot of people. Jesus frames righteousness in what the Law (Torah) and the Prophets of the Old Testament said: a right relationship with God and a right relationship with others. Perhaps some suffered from a shallow understanding of the definition or had mixed it with some conventional wisdom. Jesus was saying obvious things like murderers are liable to face God's judgment, and that adultery was wrong. Who would disagree with that? But then he would cut unexpectedly deep and say, "But I say to you that if you are angry with a brother or sister, you will be liable to judgment (5:22), and, "But I say to you that everyone who looks at a woman with lust has already committed adultery with her in his heart (5:28)."

Righteousness, to Jesus, the Law, and the Prophets was/is not about what's performative, such as how an actor performs in a

---

18. Williard, *The Divine Conspiracy*, 111.

play. Righteousness was/is a matter of character, of who a person is from the inside out. We can also think of it in light of what Jesus says later on in Matthew in an interaction with a lawyer:

> And one of them, an expert in the law, asked him [Jesus] a question to test him. "Teacher, which commandment in the law is the greatest?" Jesus said to him, "'You shall love the Lord your God with all your heart and with all your soul and with all your mind.' This is the greatest and first commandment. And a second is like it: 'You shall love your neighbor as yourself.' On these two commandments hang all the Law and the Prophets. (Matt 22:37–40)

Righteousness has to do with a person's whole self and their devotion to God. They are laying every part of themselves at God's feet and entirely dependent on him. But the reciprocal love between God and us means it's also relational and should impact our relationships with everyone, even our supposed enemies. Jesus, then, says we'll know a righteous person if they bear good fruit—the character of the kingdom of God. All who submit themselves to this type of righteousness produced by the wisdom of God, no matter their earthly station, can experience a foretaste of the kingdom to come while preparing to live in the eternal kingdom that can rule in their hearts in the present.

Jesus ends his sermon by giving a promise and a warning. Those who apply his words beyond surface-level observance act with and in God's wisdom. He doesn't promise that his disciples and other listeners won't face tribulation but that those who act according to God's wisdom can withstand their trials. The warning is for those who fail to act and be formed by his wisdom, who wish to keep with the conventional wisdom of the day, which is subject to change, and remain foolish. The late Tim Keller provides us with a better understanding of how a fool is understood in the Bible:

> Foolishness is gullibility. "The simple believe anything" (Prov 14:15). They are too easily led and influenced. Like children, they may be overimpressed by the spectacular and dramatic, or they may need approval too much and so be taken in by forceful personalities who give it to

them. They will support dictatorial leaders who promise them peace and prosperity. They can be intellectually lazy, not wanting to ponder and think out a matter. They are also likely to fall for get-rich-quick schemes (12:11).[19]

With that definition in mind, we can easily understand what Jesus meant when he said that rejecting his teaching, which is rejecting God's wisdom, is foolish and that that person's life is like a house built on sand. When that person's life falls, "great is its fall" (Matt 7:26–27)! Therefore, the fool doesn't have access to the kingdom of God in this life or the next. Here again, Jesus' kingliness shines through as "the crowds were astounded at his teaching, for he taught them as one having authority and not as their scribes" (7:28–29).

HIGH PRIEST JESUS

Additionally, Jesus' humanity epitomizes the repeated biblical statement that *God is with us*. This is what it means for him to recover our priestly status and to take the role of High Priest. Being made in the image of God meant that we were also God's representatives to creation; we were meant to present what God looks like and direct all of creation to him, and Adam and Eve's uncorrupted union with God made that possible. Adam and Eve, however, failed in their priestly duties, just as they had failed in their royal duties, choosing to worship themselves. When they decided to worship themselves, it created a rift in humanity's understanding of what they need to be themselves, to be in union or at-one with God. And that sin bound us to death just as God had warned Adam it would (Gen 2:17).

Even so, God was still content to be with us, giving Israel tangible evidence of his presence, such as descending on the Tabernacle in a cloud of glory. Still, in our misdirected attempt to honor him, we housed him away in a temple. I say we, not just Israel, because we are all guilty sometimes of putting God in a box.

---

19. Keller and Keller, *God's Wisdom*, 9.

However, God will not be contained or stand for being misrepresented. Humanity needed a true representative of who God is and to show us how to worship God, as well as how to participate in God's life and what that means for our humanity. All of that is found in the priestly role of Jesus.

In terms of worship, for example, The gospel of Luke, in chapter 17, shows an encounter between Jesus and a Samaritan. Regarding how worship is viewed, Luke provides a window into the different understandings of worship between the Samaritans and Jews. Earlier in chapter 9 of Luke, Jesus "set his face towards Jerusalem" (Luke 9:51), which can be seen as a jab against the Samaritans. Commentators like Dennis Hamm suggested that the "jab" is why the Samaritan village rejected him and the disciples. The Samaritans believed that they had the correct place for the Temple to worship God at Mount Gerizim and that to worship in Jerusalem was heretical.[20] Therefore, the Samaritans resented Jewish pilgrims on the road to Jerusalem who would pass them by.[21] Similarly, it's much the same between religions such as Christianity and Islam or Christianity and Judaism regarding where worship should be directed. However, Jesus uses the outcast to change how the religious see things, whether those eyewitnesses are people like the disciples or the reader.

Continuing on, as Jesus is traveling to Jerusalem, he comes to a village where a group of ten lepers greet him while maintaining their distance (Luke 17:11–12). As the story unfolds, and as they recognize the authority of Jesus, they ask for healing, and then Jesus promptly tells them to go before the priests. The ten men realized they were healed on their journey to the priests (17:13–14). However, only the man identified as the Samaritan returned to Christ and glorified God because of what happened (17:14–15). In fact, the Samaritan prostrated himself, bowed face down on his hands and knees, at the feet of Jesus. This is significant because the New Testament uses the posture as one that implies worship, and mainly, being at the feet of someone is recognition of seeing them

---

20. Hamm, "What the Samaritan Leper Sees," 276.
21. Hamm, "What the Samaritan Leper Sees," 282.

BEHOLD THE MAN!

as authoritative.[22] This account in Luke is about true worship, who to worship, and where to worship. Luke shows that where one worships God changes from the temples to the feet of Jesus.[23] More importantly, however, it shows how the ministry of Jesus transforms a person like this Samaritan, the "outsider."

Moreover, the Samaritan was the one to see his healing take place and the one who had a genuine desire to worship God because of it. Nevertheless, his only reaction was to glorify God. Luke's identification of the man as a Samaritan informs the reader that the man should be viewed in a context that Jesus is drawing all humanity to himself (John 12:32). It must be considered then that those in other faiths who dialogue with Christians have a genuine desire to worship, even if Christians believe they do not worship correctly. More importantly, if Christians take the transformative ministry of Jesus seriously, they may be able to lead others in differing faiths to true worship in Christ.

This would mean that the priestliness of Christ is relational, and it is. Through Jesus, we get to personally know God. Relationships create knowledge in the one sharing and receiving the knowledge. Dr. Cheryl Bridges Johns refers to such as a reordering of gathering knowledge that calls upon the Hebrew word *yada*.[24] The knowledge informed by a relationship is based on knowing through the heart rather than just through the head and conveys an engagement through lived experience.[25] It takes on an ethical tone because the dynamics of *yada* are measured through love and response rather than subject and object.[26] The purpose of this knowledge is revelatory in nature. In a biblical sense, it reveals both the heart of God and the one seeking God. It also shows the glory of God, which is his beauty and holiness, and reveals humanity's

---

22. Hamm, "What the Samaritan Leper Sees," 283–284.

23. Hamm, "What the Samaritan Leper Sees," 284.

24. Usually, and way too often, *Yada* only gets attention for its connotation of sexual intimacy.

25. Johns, "From Babel to Pentecost," 138.

26. Johns, "From Babel to Pentecost," 138.

sinfulness.[27] In a human sense, *yada* knowledge can forge deep bonds between one person and another.

Both Testaments of the biblical text signify the overall importance of the *yada* knowledge humanity is to have of God. There are, however, explicit examples in Jesus' ministry that display this more concretely. For instance, in John's gospel, Jesus' interaction with the woman at the well is one of those occurrences. Almost immediately, the woman's identification as a Samaritan is given by both her and the narrator when Jesus asks her for a drink (John 4:8–9). It is not only her heritage that makes her stand out, but also her gender.[28] It is neither explicit nor implicit that Jesus knows why she is drawing the water. Yet, after Jesus requests the drink, he moves into the beginning stages of revealing who he is and giving the woman a chance to respond, showing where her mind is dwelling. The critical thing to remember is that Christ is starting out this relational experience by starting with where she's at before bringing her to the revelation of who he is.[29] This speaks to her need to draw water and her situation beyond the well, her relational experiences highlighted in terms of her marriages (4:10–15, 17–18). Through Christ's continuing interaction with her, though, she begins to understand his identity through the offer of living water and his prophetic understanding of her multiple marriages.

Two things happen at this point between Christ and the Samaritan woman. The first is that recalling the leper from Luke, Jesus doesn't point to Mount Gerizim or the Temple in Jerusalem as the site of true worship; it's in worshiping him, as those who worship God in Spirit will recognize.[30] The second is that through the process of the *yada* knowledge, Christ's role as the Messiah is revealed to her. Again, like the previous example from Luke, the ministry of Christ transforms the person's view of worship, and the glory of God is revealed. In this instance, however, the woman can't help herself to go and witness to others and bring them to Christ

27. Johns, "From Babel to Pentecost," 138.
28. Brodie, *The Gospel According to John*, 221.
29. Brodie, *The Gospel According to John*, 221.
30. Brodie, *The Gospel According to John*, 223.

Behold The Man!

both physically and because of her testimony (4:28–30, 39–42). The revelation the woman had through a relational process had a contagious effect on other relationships.

We can't ignore the personal significance of what Jesus is doing here with the woman at the well. It's a picture of the mission of what the true priesthood was supposed to be doing:

> A covenant people, a light to the nations, to open the eyes that are blind, to bring out the prisoners from the dungeon, from the prison those who sit in darkness, that my salvation may reach to the end of the earth. (Isa 42:6–7, 49:6)

Jesus pointing the unnamed woman to true worship was not about God selfishly lavishing attention upon himself to somehow grow in power. His offer to her of a "spring of water gushing up to eternal life" (John 4:14), points us back to the union we once shared with God, who is the source of our life, and how that radically transforms our lives as his children. The lack of worshipping God vertically manifests horizontally. This means our lack of knowing and following God shows up in how we treat those around us. Jesus' physical presence, the real-world manifestation of God with us, declares what no ritual in the temple could re-produce. That is, worshipping God in Christ Jesus can heal our relationship with the God who formed us, heal our relationships with others, and heal us from the damages we've sustained in relationships.

Jesus' portrait of worship with the woman at the well demonstrates that God is our true husband. We find out in the passage that the woman has had five husbands and is not married to the man she's with now (4:16–18). Depending on the person and how they read this exchange, we could reasonably believe the Samaritan woman was an adulterer. However, given the context of her time and that men didn't need many grounds to divorce their wives, she was most likely the victim of her failed marriages. However, Jesus would be the one man who could never disappoint her. This fact is revealed in her growing understanding that the flesh and blood person standing in front of her, who knew details about her life even though she'd never seen him before, was the Messiah who

The Garden of Scripture

"is coming" and who would "proclaim all things to us" (4:25). In Jesus, with both his kingliness and his priesthood, God proclaims who he is and calls us back to the One who loved us first so we can be reconciled.

The cross is where God chose to make our ultimate reconciliation with him happen. Perhaps now is a good time to return to the question I mentioned in the first chapter, which my friend asks from time to time: what happened on the cross? But even before we get into that, I want to do something weird and talk about the early twentieth-century author H. P. Lovecraft.

The deceased author came to fame for his stories centered on cosmic horror, and he significantly influenced later authors like Stephen King and Alan Moore. In Lovecraft's stories, such as *At The Mountains of Madness,* the characters find themselves in forgotten places of the world and see things that break their sanity. In other stories, like *The Call of Cthulhu,* characters are up against evil cults who worship monstrous beings from the unsearched cosmos who rule over long-dead civilizations, seeking to rise again. Although they haven't aged well because of ridiculous racist tropes, Lovecraft's tales admittedly create a captivating air of mystery and suspense that form a sense of dread at the thought of real-life ancient and cosmic settings, almost wanting these stories to be true while not wanting to face the terror of its possibility.

All of the best literature is like that in some way. Perhaps good stories are more like a debate. Author Jason M. Baxter, who is also a professor, tells his students:

> ... the goal in arguing with someone is not to convince them but it's to make them sad that what you said is not true if they decide to walk away from the conversation ... you can at least make your interlocuter feel at the end of the conversation think, "Wow, even if that's not true, I kind of wish it were."[31]

The Gospel is like this, presenting a beautiful picture of redemption through a God who, as it turns out, actually *does* love

---

31. Stanford and Banks, "Medieval Mind of C. S. Lewis."

BEHOLD THE MAN!

humanity, who *wants* to raise us out of the muck we purposely walked into to *deliver* us from the oppression of sin, death, and ourselves, and *gives* the life of his only begotten Son to secure this destiny. However, the benefit of the Gospel over all other great literature is that it has the advantage of being true.

Similarly, although the message that the promised salvation declared by God in the Hebrew Scriptures is true and that the promise is now going to be fulfilled is beautiful, there is a type of terror that confronts us. The anxiety of this terror is built through encounters like Simeon's and Anna's with the newborn Jesus and his parents in Jerusalem's Temple. "This child is destined for the falling and the rising of many in Israel," Simeon says to Mary after he praises God. For Jesus, it is "to be a sign that will be opposed so that the inner thoughts of many will be revealed." If that is not enough, Simeon ensures that the conversation with Mary, the mother of Jesus, doesn't end on a comfortable note, saying, "and a sword will pierce your own soul, too" (Luke 2:34–35). The prophetess Anna, who never leaves the temple, ratchets up the anxiety by testifying to everyone in proximity about how Jesus would bring about the redemption of Jerusalem (2:37–38).

Jesus only adds to the nervous anticipation. During his ministry, he would travel around saying, "Repent, for the Kingdom of heaven is at hand" (Matt 4:17), and follow that up by healing, casting out demons, and confronting oppressive religious traditions. The anxiety that was built up by Anna and Simeon at the beginning of Jesus' life is mirrored by the closing of his ministry, where we find that he drew such large crowds the Pharisees and Priests are afraid to arrest him because of them (Matt 21:46, John 11:45–53).

On the other hand, we must qualify the terror and dread of the Gospel. We can't say, as we could with Lovecraft, that the anxiety Jesus creates results in unfathomable terror. Noticeably, the kind of anxiety he produced led to joy. As I hinted above, the Gospel was founded in hope. We find this hope in places like the Psalms, where it says, "The Lord is near to the brokenhearted and saves the crushed in spirit" (Ps. 34:18), and in the prophets, where

The Garden of Scripture

it says, "He will swallow up death forever; and the Lord God will wipe away tears from all faces" (Isa 25:8), and "A new heart I will give you, and a new spirit I will put within you, and I will remove from your body the heart of stone and give you a heart of flesh" (Ezek 36:26), along with many others. The people who encountered Jesus in the spirit of these verses saw their hopes fulfilled. So, whereas devoted readers of Lovecraft almost want his stories to be true while not wanting to face the terror of its possibility, those who followed Jesus became part of a story that is true and embraced the joy of its reality.

At the same time, the Gospel does contain an iota of horror experienced by us and other entities. The villains in the gospels are sometimes human. We like to point to Judas and the religious authorities, who were full of betrayal and envy. Sometimes, however, people were villainous only at the moment, like when Peter "took him aside and began to rebuke him, saying, 'God forbid it, Lord! This must never happen to you'" after Jesus prophesied about his own death (Matt 16:22). But the real villains, are sin, death and the devil (Heb 2:15, 1 John 3:8b). It's sin that is like the Lovecraftian terror, with twisting tentacles that hold us in bondage from which Satan introduced into humanity with the deception that God is keeping us from secret knowledge; as John wrote, the devil has been sinning from the beginning (1 John 3:8a). Thus, we become villainous when we give in to sin and are capable of committing all sorts of terror against each other, even to the point of crucifying the Son of God. Yet, it is sin, death, and the devil who experience the absolute terror as the end nears.

Let's now return to the question, "What happened on the cross?" We can say that Jesus entered into his ultimate act as High Priest, not performing a sacrifice but offering himself up as *the* sacrifice that takes away the sin of the world (John 1:29). Christian theology makes much of this event called the atonement, and rightly so, offering many theories of why it happened and what it accomplished.[32] Some get wound up in trying to determine which one is correct, but as C. S. Lewis stated in his book *Mere Christianity*,

---

32. There are at least six well known theories of atonement.

"A man can accept what Christ has done without knowing how it works: indeed, he certainly would not know how it works until he has accepted it."[33] I admit, however, that we are approaching it from having accepted it, and to understand it better, especially in terms of what Jesus as High Priest means for our humanity, we must explore it.

The cross happened, to state again, because Adam, whose name indicates the original name of the original man,[34] failed in his priestly duties, representing the image of God to creation. Being that he embodied the whole human race, the wholeness of humanity was impacted by sin.[35] This is why the Apostle Paul called Jesus the "second Adam." At several crucial points in his life and ministry, Jesus' faithful obedience to his Father redeemed the disobedience of Adam and Israel, events that the church-father Irenaeus called recapitulation. Through his sin, Adam's priesthood led to the entrance of death for humanity, but as High Priest, Jesus enters into death and ushers in eternal life for humanity through his resurrection (Rom 5:12–15). Since a critical component of humanity is being flesh and blood, Christ's sacrifice needed to be done in the flesh. As Patrick Henry Reardon states,

> It is precisely because Christ is the replacement of Adam that Christ can be no less human than Adam, composed of both soul and body. As the whole human being fell in Adam, the whole human being was restored in Christ.[36]

So, then Jesus, as priest and king, rescues the totality of humans. Through the ultimate act of humility, not only are our sins completely forgiven, but the restoration of our relationship with God means that we can be truly human, which is to be in union with God as co-sons and daughters with Christ.

Finally, as High Priest, Jesus completely reorients the structure of the Temple. In Revelation 21, the author is granted a vision

---

33. Lewis, *Mere Christianity*, 55.
34. Reardon, *Reclaiming the Atonement*, 147.
35. Reardon, *Reclaiming the Atonement*, 147
36. Reardon, *Reclaiming the Atonement*, 147, 155.

of the new heaven and earth with the New Jerusalem descending into view. In one beautiful line, the author writes, "See, the home of God is among mortals" (Rev 21:3b). A lot is happening with this passage, more than we have space for here, but one thing we can say about it is that we are treated to a vision of a restored reality. No longer are the spiritual and physical realms distinct spheres in our understanding, nor are they like two circles on a Venn diagram converging; they are totally engulfed in one another.

In the following verses, John, the author, describes the construction of New Jerusalem, which is made of transparent gold and adorned with the twelve jewels that mark the tribes of Israel. He is also given the city's measurements, which are said to resemble a perfect cube. All of those images are important for one reason or another, but John makes another significant observation, "I saw no temple in the city, for its temple is the Lord God the Almighty and the Lamb" (21:22). God wants to be with us, and no temple can indeed hold him, so he himself is the true Temple where all things are united to him existing eternally.

As I mentioned, all this confirms that *God is with* and *for us*. In reflecting on Jesus' recovery of our humanity, I am reminded of a quote by Portuguese Jesuit priest Joao Rodrigues, the novelist James Clavell made famous in this novel *Shōgun*. Commenting on the supposed mystery of the Japanese people when he lived among them, Rodrigues states the Japanese have three hearts,

> A false one in their mouths for all the world to see, another within their breasts only for their friends, and third in the depths of their hearts, reserved for themselves alone and never manifested to anyone.[37]

The difference, of course, is that Jesus is the manifested innermost heart of God, whom he revealed to everyone. Since Christ has redeemed and made perfect what it means to be human, we can reflect the kingdom of God, which we will one-day co-rule, and take part in the priesthood of Jesus by pointing others to him.

---

37. Rodrigues SJ, *História da Igreja do Japão*, 173.

8

An Invitation To Slay Dragons

Holiness is preeminently expressed in love; and love is the essential means by which holiness is maintained. To love others is to refuse to use them for selfish ends or to take advantage of them.

—J. Ayodeji Adewuya[1]

REFLECTING BACK ON MY college-aged years, I remember feeling excited at being invited to my first parties. It was significant because I was new to the area (Massachusetts), and we had many common interests, such as Star Trek, the Beatles, acting, and other nerdy things. I felt accepted for who I was, and they had a way of drawing me out of my shell instead of forcing me out. I wasn't good at denying temptation, though, and a lot of stuff spun out of control and caused a lot of problems. When I talk to my oldest child, who's rapidly approaching the age I was during those times, it's not enough to say that he should avoid the same temptations; he needs to know the emotional and psychological toll giving into temptation can take on a person, the toll it took on me and how some of that pain can still be felt a lifetime later. Even so, as bad as things became, I sometimes wish that some of the people I've met

---

1. Adewuya, *Holiness in the Letters of Paul*, 161.

along the way who share my faith were and are as accepting and inviting as my college friends were.

Christ's life was a demonstration of the divine and an invitation into it. It's the invitation to participate in God's divine, holy life. How does that sound? Is it better than the version of Christianity sometimes offered in the West, the kind parodied by *The Simpsons* with the character of Ned Flanders? The Bible is ordered, but not so ordered, that it presents a safe, palatable, and even bland faith. Not much is safe about a faith whose Lord says, "If any wish to come after me, let them deny themselves and take up their cross daily and follow me. For those who want to save their life will lose it, and those who lose their life for my sake will save it" (Luke 9:23–24). For some, Jesus' words are or will be literal; if they choose to follow Jesus, they will lose their lives because they will have been martyred. But the Gospel and the rest of the New Testament teach that losing our lives means our characters and behaviors are wholly transformed by believing in Christ and accepting his invitation to be like him.

CHANGING CLOTHES

But let's be realistic, the continuing process of salvation, which can be termed sanctification, doesn't happen overnight. This is because there are things that must be unlearned so that we can learn what it means to follow Christ. We can call this being "undragoned," a term C. S. Lewis gives us in his Narnia book *The Voyage of the Dawn Treader* with the character Eustace. Early in the book, Eustace, cousin to Edmund and Lucy, is said to embody dragonish characteristics such as anger, greediness, and bitterness. These traits are personified when his behaviors lead him to transform into an actual dragon. Throughout the story, Eustace begins to loathe himself in his new body. When he reaches an especially low point as a dragon, he meets the lion Aslan, who invites him into a mountain garden to transform him back into a human. It's in the garden where Eustace sees a large bath. Recounting to his cousin Edmund, Eustace tells him, "the water was as clear as anything and

An Invitation To Slay Dragons

I thought if I could just get in there and bathe, it would ease the pain in my leg. But the lion told me I must undress first."[2]

The undressing, of course, meant that Eustace had to shed his dragon skin. With every attempt to shed the scales, he only finds more underneath the ones he'd just torn off with his claws. After the third failed attempt, it is revealed that only Aslan can remove Eustace's scales.[3] Although Eustace is scared of Aslan's claws, he agrees and lays on his back, waiting for the Lion's claws. For anyone who hasn't read the book, it's at this time where we would like to think that Aslan, a representation of Jesus, didn't hurt Eustace, but that is not what we get. Eustace explains,

> The very first tear he made was so deep that I thought it had gone right into my heart. And when he began pulling the skin off, it hurt worse than anything I've ever felt. The only thing that made me able to bear it was just the pleasure of feeling the stuff peel off. You know—if you've ever picked the scab off a sore place. It hurts like a billy-oh but it is such fun to see it coming away.[4]

Lewis's scene with Eustace is a prime example of how the New Testament writers speak about Christ's continuing salvific work. In Lewisian terms, Christ's sacrifice on the cross was the moment the great undragoning of the world began. "The only way back to the garden is through the tomb," the saying goes. The resurrection of Christ, though, proves he has undragoned us because he has slain the dragon of death, which sin had bound us to. It is the work of Christ's followers to be a sign of that process and to show that we have been undragoned by Christ. As with Eustace, the process of sanctification can be painful because we have to continually yield to the work of the Spirit and apply the crucifixion to our lives. It can mean we must let go of things we thought made us strong, like "enmity, strife, jealousy, anger, quarrels, dissensions, factions, and envy (Gal 5:20–21)," but they really made us monsters.

---

2. Lewis, *Dawn Treader*, 58.
3. Lewis, *Dawn Treader*, 59.
4. Lewis, *Dawn Treader*, 59.

The Garden of Scripture

Eustace's undragoning didn't end after Aslan removed all the scales. After they are removed, Aslan catches hold of him and throws him into the garden bath, which he says, "smarted like anything but only for a moment."[5] Some things still need to be accomplished in the "working out of our salvation" that may be unpleasant. But just as Eustace begins to swim in the bath, discovering it to be pleasurable and even healing, Christians find that the sustaining work of Christ in the power of the Spirit renews us continuously and brings us to the state we were created to be. This is why we have the letters we have in the New Testament. Although Jesus' atonement is completed on the cross, the understanding of that work and its application must be surrendered to daily by us. "Those who belong to Christ have crucified the flesh with its passions and desires," Paul says (Gal 5:24). We're going to have trouble with this; the Bible is fully aware of it. However, the appeal of the New Testament writers is that the process is livable and that the working out of salvation can and must be done.

Yielding doesn't have to be too difficult because Jesus supplies us with what we need to succeed. He does this by giving us the Holy Spirit as our advocate, and we are told we can live by the Spirit if we let him guide us (Gal 5:25, John 14:16). When that happens, it's like receiving a new wardrobe. Consider Eustace's story again; after he recounts his bath to his cousin Edmund, Eustace says that Aslan dresses him, "I don't exactly remember that bit. But he did somehow or other, in new clothes. . ."[6] However, that is precisely what Christ does for us, as Scripture details. In Paul's letter to the church in Rome, he tells his hearers to "put on the Lord Jesus Christ," which mirrors what he says to those in Colossae that "as God's chosen ones, holy and beloved, clothe yourselves with compassion, kindness, humility, meekness, and patience" (Rom 13:14, Col 3:12). We are to clothe ourselves in Christ.

---

5. Lewis, *Dawn Treader*, 59.
6. Lewis, *Dawn Treader*, 60.

AN INVITATION TO SLAY DRAGONS

GROWTH IN CHRIST

The purpose of putting on Christ is to assume his identity. The word "identity" is primarily in a Christian context. The word "Christian" itself signifies that it has an end goal, what the Greeks would call *telos*. The philosopher Aristotle used an acorn as an example. The acorn's goal is to become an oak tree since it stores the potential within it to become an oak. We know that all acorns will become oak trees because when they are planted, they grow into oak trees. Therefore, when we identify as Christians, we should not only claim the name of Jesus, but who he is and who he has proven to be should inhabit every part of our lives with the end goal of being like Jesus and with Jesus. That is why the followers of Jesus who fled to Antioch were the first ones to be called Christians; they claimed Christ's identity through their actions, living and loving as he instructed (Acts 11:26). It's what the Apostle Paul means when he says, "I have been crucified with Christ; it is no longer I who live, but it is Christ who lives in me" (Gal 2:20).

To imply that our faith is like an acorn that turns into its final form suggests that our faith must grow. Paul understood this when he wrote to the believers in Corinth, whose members had trouble letting some things go, stating, "I fed you with milk, not solid food, for you were not ready for solid food. Even now you are still not ready" (1 Cor 3:2). The Apostle Peter, too, talks about growth, using a different milk metaphor, saying, "Like newborn infants, long for the pure, spiritual milk, so that by it you may grow into salvation" (1 Peter 2:2). Even the author of Hebrews gets in on the fun, telling his readers, "You need milk, not solid food; for everyone who lives on milk, still being an infant, is unskilled in the word of righteousness. Solid food is for the mature" (Heb 5:12b–14a).

AN ETHICAL CALLING

The reason for the Apostle's comments on maturity is to highlight the need to learn how to be humble like Christ and how to love as he did. Christians are like the little Swallow from Oscar Wilde's

The Happy Prince. If you're unfamiliar with Wilde's story, it centers on a golden statue of a prince perched high atop a column in the middle of an unnamed Northern European city. Very early on in the tale, a Swallow flew to the same city on his migratory trip to Egypt stopping to rest and finding the statue as a good place to shelter.[7] Feeling good about having a "golden bedroom," he suddenly feels a drop of water and gets aggravated that such a statue can't even keep water off him. As he is about to fly off in annoyance, he notices that the eyes of the statue are filled with tears.

Over a short conversation, the Swallow learns that the Prince was once a real-life person who never had to want for anything, never suffered, or even saw suffering. As a statue, however, the Prince can see the whole city and all those who experience poverty and sorrow.[8] At the moment of the conversation, the golden Prince sees someone in need, and being bound to the column, he invites the Swallow to act, bringing a jewel from his golden sword to mother and her son, who's been suffering from a fever for days. But, you know, that request doesn't really align with the Swallow's plans. He's on a time crunch and has to meet with his friends who are flying up and down the Nile, and he actually doesn't like human boys because a few of them were mean to him once, so it's just not a convenient time right now.[9] Yet, the Swallow was moved by the statue's piteous face; he agreed to stay another night with the statue despite the cold and be his messenger by bringing a jewel to the people in need. Two unintended things happened when the Swallow delivered the jewel. First, flapping his wings cooled the boy's head as he flew around the room, allowing him to fall asleep. Second, upon his return to the Prince, the Swallow remarked, "It is curious . . . I feel quite warm now, although it is so cold,"[10] an obvious sign of his heart being stirred.

It may be apparent by now, but we can say that the golden statue of the Happy Prince is a picture of Christ. Although the

---

7. Wilde, *The Happy Prince*, 15.
8. Wilde, *The Happy Prince*, 17–18.
9. Wilde, *The Happy Prince*, 20.
10. Wilde, *The Happy Prince*, 22.

An Invitation To Slay Dragons

analogy of the Prince as a portrait of Jesus isn't perfect, it speaks well enough to the progression of spiritual maturity in a salvific relationship with him. Unlike the statue, Christ is not fixed but asks us to continue his work. This multifaceted "work" of Jesus, to "bring good news to the poor, to release the captives, recover the sight of the blind, to let the oppressed go free and proclaim the year of the Lord's favor" (Luke 4:18) is infused with love but in a way is meant to stretch us and form us, which can be seen as inconvenient by many.

Claiming the morality of what Christianity teaches alone does not entirely represent the Christian identity. Much to the discomfort of some, what we find in the letters of the New Testament are the authors claiming that when Jesus said, "Truly I tell you, just as you did it to one of the least of these brothers and sisters of mine, you did it to me" (Matt 25:40), he meant it. We do need to help provide for each other (Acts 4:32-36). We do need to look after the widows (Acts 6, James 1:27). We do need to bring the Gospel to the Other (Acts 10, 15). We do need to engage with those who seem "lower" than us (Rom 12:16). We do need to come before the Lord as a united and equal body (Gal 3:28, 1 Cor 11:17-22, 12:26, 1 John 3:11, etc.). The Apostle John says this is not accomplished through mere speech but in "*truth* and *action*" (3:18).

Sometimes, even for the first Christians, the topic of charitable action must be stated bluntly. James, the author of his own epistle, shares it like this:

> What good is it, my brothers and sisters, if someone claims to have faith but has no deeds? Can such faith save them? Suppose a brother or a sister is without clothes and daily food. If one of you says to them, "Go in peace; keep warm and well fed," but does nothing about their physical needs, what good is it? In the same way, faith by itself, if it is not accompanied by action, is dead. But someone will say, "You have faith; I have deeds." Show me your faith without deeds, and I will show you my faith by my deeds. You believe that there is one God. Good! Even the demons believe that—and shudder. (James 2:14-19, NIV)

The Garden of Scripture

If that passage is not straightforward enough, James finishes his statements by saying, "As the body without the spirit is dead, so faith without deeds is dead" (2:26).

Again, though, the action takes humility. Humility is simply placing the needs of others higher than ourselves. The more we humble ourselves, the more we face the cost of that humility. We can look again at the story of *The Happy Prince* to see an example of this. A day after he delivers the jewel, the statue asks the Swallow to take a sapphire representing one of his eyes. The bird protests and begins to weep, and somewhat shockingly, the Prince replies, "Swallow, Swallow, little Swallow, do as I command you."[11] Perhaps the cost to the little bird was having to take something precious from something so beautiful, which would seem to cause the beauty to be lessened, and having to deal with those emotions. One of the things about acting benevolently on behalf of Christ is that the one receiving the benevolence won't always respond in the way we wish they would. They may accept what is given without accepting Christ. Indeed, the one who received the sapphire thought an admirer of his work snuck it into his room and nothing more.

The other part of the cost we must consider is that Christ calls his followers to be continually benevolent. This is because, as Paul writes to Titus, "these things are excellent and profitable to everyone (Titus 3:8)." However, our good works may not be profitable in ways we generally envision. In a moving scene toward the end of *The Happy Prince*, we see how that profitability plays out. After several more instances of "good work" on behalf of the golden Prince, the love of the Swallow towards the Prince grew to the point where he would not leave him despite the harsh winter about to set in. As the story draws to a close, the reader finds that the Prince has been stripped of the gold leaf covering his body. The once-golden prince says to the bird,

> "I am glad that you are going to Egypt at last, little Swallow," said the Prince, "you have stayed too long here; but you must kiss me on the lips, for I love you."

---

11. Wilde, *The Happy Prince*, 26.

AN INVITATION TO SLAY DRAGONS

"It is not to Egypt that I am going," said the Swallow. "I am going to the House of Death. Death is the brother of Sleep, is he not?"

And he kissed the Happy Prince on the lips, and fell down dead at his feet.[12]

With this example, I'm not intending to say that true Christian benevolence requires the sacrifice of our physical lives to be considered as something profitable, although for some, that may come to pass (Rom 5:8, John 15:13). What we do need to recognize, however, is that a continual Christian ethic and the doing of good works demonstrated by the New Testament does lead to a type of profitable death,[13] the death of our selfishness. When our selfishness dies, we come to love in the way our self-giving God does and love him the more for it.

RECIPROCAL MORALITY

As much as the death of selfishness relates to Christian ethics, it's also related to Christian morality. Some believe that acting with a certain charity toward our neighbor should be enough to be considered a good representative of Christianity. The problem with such a limited view is that the New Testament writers never separate the moral and ethical. Doing what is right and good is framed or seen through the lens of Christ, and so being good in mind and body must also be done through the same lens. We must identify, though, how Jesus and the New Testament writers define morality.

In the previous chapter, I claimed that Jesus defined righteousness in the tradition of the Torah and the prophets. The same is true for morality. Both Jesus and the Apostles continued to define morality in the same tradition. The Ten Commandments are as follows:

---

12. Wilde, *The Happy Prince*, 33–34.

13. Christian ethics are the doing of good, which benevolence and charity falls under. Doing what's right, such as standing up for the oppressed (Prov. 30:8–9), also falls under Christian ethics.

The Garden of Scripture

> You shall have no other gods before Me.
> You shall not make idols.
> You shall not take the name of the LORD your God in vain.
> Remember the Sabbath day, to keep it holy.
> Honor your father and your mother.
> You shall not murder.
> You shall not commit adultery.
> You shall not steal.
> You shall not bear false witness against your neighbor.
> You shall not covet your neighbor's possessions.
> (Exod 20:1–17)

Whether we like it or not, this list is still relevant to the Christian life. Jesus, in fact, in the Sermon on the Mount, expounds on the wisdom of these commandments, tying them to the very core of human behavior.

In the Apostle Paul's letters, he explains what is immoral regarding behaviors that are part of "the flesh," which means behaviors born out of fallen human nature. We see these most famously displayed in Galatians 5, where Paul says, "Now the works of the flesh are obvious: sexual immorality, moral impurity, promiscuity, idolatry, sorcery, hatreds, strife, jealousy, outbursts of anger, selfish ambitions, dissensions, factions, envy, drunkenness, carousing, and anything similar" (Gal 5:19–21a, CSB). Annoyingly to some, he also teaches in Ephesians that followers of Christ should make sure that "no foul language come out of your mouth, but only what is good for building up someone in need" (Eph 4:29).

There is a world wherein Paul's command to avoid cussing someone out might seem nitpicky, but he says so for a more profound reason than we may realize. His follow-up of "but only what is good for building up someone in need" is directly tied to the Greek word used for foul, *sapros*. The word literally translates to rotten, and its root word, *sepo*, means decay and is where we get the words for sepsis and septic. In your mind, imagine a rotten piece of fruit, a crumbling building, or a stream of sewage, and you may have an idea of what Paul was getting at. Foul words and speaking foully of another person are directly opposed to the Christian faith because they are meant to, in an emotional and psychological

An Invitation To Slay Dragons

context, take life away. Christians are a people, however, who worship Jesus, who gives us life and gives it abundantly through the giving of his own life (John 10:10). Not only that, but by being indwelled with the Spirit of God, we can participate in God's very own life. So, when we permit ourselves to use such foul language or speak foully of another, we act as agents of decay instead of grace, acting against the life given to us and offered to others.

The issue of decay and foulness isn't just about saying potty words; it speaks to the very issue of immorality as a whole, an anti-life. As immoral as it is to cuss someone out, things like cheating on your taxes, presenting another's work as your own to get a promotion, lusting after dressed and undressed bodies, sleeping with someone other than your spouse, fleeing the scene of an accident to avoid prosecution or having to pay higher insurance, scamming people to empty their bank accounts to fund a "ministry," to think or say racist things, etc., all fall under the umbrella of what the New Testament writers call immorality. This is because they all have decaying consequences for ourselves and others that contradict the life Christ calls us to lead.

We can see by now that being moral is not just for the benefit of our relationship with God; it also benefits our relationships with others. It has always been this way and is reflected in the Ten Commandments, which scholars say are relationally vertical and horizontal. So, how we think, act, and speak toward ourselves and others is a good indicator of our relationship with the Triune God and vice versa. We can also say that if we stray from the first two Commandments, "You shall have no other gods before Me" and "You shall not make idols," it's easy to violate the rest because immorality stems from making ourselves a god.

So, becoming moral is a part of the undragoning. There is no "just being ethical" or "just being moral," there is no half salvation in Christianity, only the whole. However, we are not expected to be paragons of Christian virtue immediately or even be perfect in the sense of never making another mistake. If that were the case, we wouldn't have the letters of the New Testament. However, we are expected to participate in what God does in our salvation

THE GARDEN OF SCRIPTURE

(Phil 2:12), yield to the Holy Spirit (Gal 5:25), and walk as Christ walked (1 John 1:6).

Jesus speaks to this concept when he teaches Matthew's parable of the wedding banquet. In the parable, a king throws a banquet for his son, who we assume has recently gotten married or is about to (Matt 22:1). He sends out messengers who request those invited to come now that everything is ready. But the invitees either dismissed the king's servants or killed them (22:3–6). After retaliating against the murderers, the king sends out additional servants who are ordered to invite whoever they meet, "both good and bad," to come and celebrate his son's wedding, resulting in a packed wedding hall (22:7–10). However, when the king arrived at the wedding hall, he noticed that one of the guests was not wearing the appropriate attire to participate in the celebrations, so he asked the guest how he got into the hall. When the guest could not answer, the king ordered his guards to throw the man out (22:11–13).

One could argue, and I do, that the closing events of the parable are "eschatological" in nature. Meaning it has to do with the return of Christ. While the wedding attire the guests wear symbolizes repentance, it also represents that they have prepared for the wedding, fulfilling the expectations of the king and showing honor to his son, identifying them as true guests.[14] The imagery also ties to the marriage supper of the Lamb we find at the end of Revelation, where the author writes, "Blessed are those who wash their robes, so that they may have the right to the tree of life and that they may enter the city by the gates (Rev 22:14). Consequently, those who may have claimed Christ during their life but still practiced the immorality outlined by Jesus and the New Testament writers are not able to enter (22:15).

CONCLUDING IMPERATIVE

To be moral, then, just like it is to be ethical, is not about being a "goody-two-shoes"; it is about being spiritually formed by Christ.

---

14. Keener, *The Gospel of Matthew*, 778.

An Invitation To Slay Dragons

However, spiritual formation, as Dallas Willard notes, "Is not about behavior modification. It is about changing the sources of behavior, so the behavior will take care of itself."[15] While we participate in our salvation, though, we must remember that it's the work of Christ that we take or put on, and he is not a taskmaster. "Take my yoke upon you, and learn from me; for I am gentle and humble in heart, and you will find rest for your souls. For my yoke is easy, and my burden is light" (Matt 11:29–30).

Christians are to do this because we are the current citizens of a kingdom that is not of this world and whose king has not yet arrived (Phil 3:20). We are a bride waiting for her groom, but if we look and act like everyone else rather than do what is necessary to get ready, how will the world know of the salvation offered by Christ and the hope to come in his kingdom? Therefore, like Eustace, we must let Christ undragon us from our old selves, giving us a new way to dress as we prepare to see him. Like the little Swallow, we must be willing to say yes to Christ's invitation to serve him as he pours himself out to the world. We must surrender to his wooing, which causes us to fall further in love with him. When we do this and finally see Jesus in his unfiltered glory upon his return, as John the Elder says, "we will be like him" (1 John 3:2).

---

15. Willard, *Living in Christ's*, 14.

Bibliography

Adewuya, J. Ayodeji. *Holiness in the Letters of Paul: The Necessary Response to the Gospel*. Eugene, OR: Cascade, 2016.
Anthony, Michael J., and Warren S. Benson. *Exploring the History and Philosophy of Christian Education: Principles for the 21st Century*. Grand Rapids: Kregel, 2003.
Barclay, William. *The Letters to the Corinthians*. Revised ed. Philadelphia: Westminster, 1975.
BBC Archive, "1962: Tolkien on Lord of the Rings: Bookstand, Writers and Wordsmiths, BBC Archive." YouTube video, January 6, 2025. 7:43. https://youtu.be/K7WulvC1lyQ?si=DbTxzLo-LrvSGaR5
Bonhoeffer, Dietrich. *Discipleship*. Edited by Geffery B Kelly and John D. Godsey. Vol. 4. Translated by Green Barbara and Reinhard Kraus. Minneapolis: Fortress, 2003.
———. *Meditating on the Word*. Translated by David McI. Grand Rapids: Baker, 2023.
Brodie, John. *The Gospel According to John: A Literary and Theological Commentary*. New York: Oxford University Press, 1997.
Bursch, Douglas S. *The Community of God: A Theology of the Church From a Reluctant Pastor*. Seatle: Fairly Spiritual, 2017.
Cabasilas, Nicolaus. *The Life in Christ*. Yonkers, NY: St. Vladimir's Seminary Press, 1997.
Calvin, John. *Institutions of Christian Religion*. Vol. 2. Grand Rapids: Eerdmans, 1975.
Culpepper, R. Alan. *The Gospel and the Letters of John*. Nashville: Abingdon, 1998.
Darabont, Frank. dir. *The Shawshank Redemption*. Screenplay by Shawn Patrick Patterson. 1994; Burbank, CA: Warner Bros., Prime Video.
Foster, Richard. *Celebrations of Discipline*. London: Hodder & Stoughton, 1989.
Gause, R. Hollis. *Hebrews: A Pentecostal Commentary*. Leiden: Brill, 2022.
Green, Chris E. W. *Sanctifying Interpretation: Vocation, Holiness, and Scripture*. 2nd ed. Cleveland, TN: CPT, 2020.
Green, Joel B. *The Gospel of Luke*. Grand Rapids: Eerdmans, 1997.
Goldingay, John. "The Breath of Yahweh Scorching, Confounding, Anointing: The Message of Isaiah 40–42." *Journal of Pentecostal Theology* 5 (Dec 1997) 3–34.

Bibliography

Hall, Christopher A. *Learning Theology with the Church Fathers*. Downers Grove: InterVarsity, 2002.

———. *Worshiping with the Church Fathers*. Downers Grove: InterVarsity, 2009.

Hamm, Dennis. "What the Samaritan Leper Sees: The Narrative Christology of Luke 17:11–19." *Catholic Bible Quarterly* (1994) 273–287.

Jerome. *Epistle 108*, CSEL 55.334. In *Reading Scripture with the Church Fathers*, by Cristopher Hall. Downers Grove: InterVarsity, 1998.

Johns, Cheryl Bridges. "From Babel to Pentecost: The Renewal of Theological Education." In *Viable Theological Education: Ecumenical Imperative, Catalyst of Renewal*, 132–146. Geneva: WCC, 1997.

———. *Re-Enchanting The Text: Discovering the Bible as Sacred, Dangerous and Mysterious.* Johnson, Luke Timothy. *The First and Second Letters to Timothy*. New York: Doubleday, 2008.

Keener, Craig S. *A Commentary on the Gospel of Matthew*. Grand Rapids: Eerdmans, 1999.

———. *Acts*. New York: Cambridge University Press, 2020.

Keller, Timothy, and Kathy Keller. *God's Wisdom for Navigating Life: A Year Of Daily Devotions in the Book of Proverbs*. New York: Viking, 2017.

Kraus, Hans-Joachim. *Theology of the Psalms*. Minneapolis: Augsburg, 1986.

Koester, Craig R. *The Word of Life: A Theology of John's Gospel*. Grand Rapids: Eerdmans, 2008

Lane, Tony. *A Concise History of Christian Thought*. Grand Rapids: Baker Academic, 2006.

Lewis, C. S. *God in the Dock*. Grand Rapids: Eerdmans, 2014.

———. *The Pilgrim's Regress*. New York: HarperOne, 2014.

———. *The Voyage of the Dawn Treader*. New York: HarperCollins, 1952.

Loconte, Joseph. *A Hobbit, a Wardrobe, and a Great War: How J. R. R. Tolkien and C. S. Lewis Rediscovered Faith, Friendship, and Heroism in the Cataclysm of 1914–1918*. Nashville: Thomas Nelson, 2015.

Lorre, Chuck, creator. *The Big Bang Theory*. Season 6, episode 21, "The Closure Alternative." Performances by Jim Parsons and Mayim Bialik. Aired April 25, 2013, on CBS. Warner Brothers, 2023, on Prime Video.

Martens, Elmer A. *God's Design: A Focus on Old Testament Theology*. 3rd ed. Eugene, OR: Wipf & Stock, 2014.

McColman, Carl. *The Big Book of Christian Mysticism: The Essential Guide to Contemplative Spirituality*. Charlottesville: Hamptons Road, 2010.

Merton, Thomas. *No Man Is an Island*. New York: Houghton Mifflin, 1983.

Odell, Margaret S. *Ezekiel: Smyth & Helwys Bible Commentary*. Macon: Smyth & Helwys Publishing, 2017.

Olson, Roger E. *The Journey of Modern Theology*. Downers Grover: InterVarsity, 2013.

Opdal, Paul Martin. "Curiosity, Wonder, and Education Seen as Perspective Development." *Studies in Philosophy and Education* 20 (2001) 331–344. https://doi.org/10.1023/A:1011851211125.

Bibliography

Prior, Karen Swallow. *The Evangelical Imagination: How Stories, Images and Metaphors Created a Culture in Crisis.* Grand Rapids: Brazos, 2023.

Reardon, Patrick Henry. *Reclaiming the Atonement: An Orthodox Theology of Redemption.* Chesterton: Ancient Faith, 2015.

Reuland, Eric. "Imagination, Planning, and Working Memory: The Emergence of Language." *Current Anthropology* 5 (2010) S99–S110.

Richie, Tony. *Essentials of Pentecostal Theology: An Eternal and Unchanging Lord Powerfully Present and Active by the Holy Spirit.* Eugene, OR: Resource, 2020.

Rodrigues, João. *Historia da Igreja do Japão.* Brazil: Noticias de Macau, 1956.

Roetzel, Calvin J. *The Letters of Paul: Conversations in Context.* 4th ed. Louisville: Westminster John Knox, 1998.

Scott Jr, J. Julius. *Jewish Backgrounds of the New Testament.* Grand Rapids: Baker Academic, 1995.

Stanford, Angelina, and Thomas Banks. "Episode 145: The Medieval Mind of C. S. Lewis: A Conversation with Jason M. Baxter." Produced by Cindy Rollins. *The Literary Life Podcast.* October 18, 2022. 1:16:23. https://theliterarylife.libsyn.com/episode-217-best-of-series-the-medieval-mind-of-c-s-lewis-a-conversation-with-jason-m-baxter-ep-145.

Sweeny, Marvin A. *Reading Ezekiel: A Literary and Theological Commentary.* Macon: Smyth & Helwys, 2013.

Tolkien, J. R. R. *The Lord of the Rings.* New York: Houghton Mifflin, 1994

———. *The Letters of J. R. R. Tolkien: Revised and Expanded Edition.* Edited by Humphrey Carpenter and Christopher Tolkien. New York: William Marrow, 2023.

Tozer, A. W. *The Knowledge of the Holy.* New York: HarperCollins, 1961.

Tschida, Tim. *The Fruit That Turns the World Upside Down: An Autobiographical and Biblical Story.* Self-Published. 2023.

Wilde, Oscar. *The Happy Prince and Other Tales.* Leipzig: Bernhard Tauchnitz, 1909.

Willard, Dallas. *The Divine Conspiracy: Rediscovering Our Hidden Life in God.* San Francisco: HarperCollins, 1997.

Wesley, John. "Sermon XXXIX: Catholic Spirit." In *The Essential Works of John Wesley*, edited by Alice Russie, 705–715. Uhrichsville, OH: Barbour, 2011.

Wright, N. T. *Matthew for Everyone: Part 1.* Louisville: Westminster John Knox, 2004.

———. *Matthew for Everyone: Part 2.* Louisville: Westminster John Knox, 2004.